VIEWS ON THE MOMENTOUS PAST OF ALLEPPEY

Views on the Momentous Past of Alleppey

BETWEEN ALAPPUZHA THEN AND ALAPPUZHA NOW

HANS SCHENK

MANOHAR
2025

First published 2025
First eBook edition 2025

ISBN 978-93-6080-271-4 (hardbound)
ISBN 978-93-6080-402-2 (eBook)

Published by

Ajay Kumar Jain *for*
Manohar Publishers & Distributors
4753/23 Ansari Road, Daryaganj
New Delhi 110 002

Cover design by Kamal Purna Jammual

Typeset by Kohli Print, Delhi 110 051

Printed and bound in India

Contents

EPILOGUE

Figures

Prologue

First, I thank the many men and women who helped me in various ways during my fieldwork in Alleppey. I wish in particular to mention the outstanding support offered during this period and thereafter by N. Gopinathan and G. Omanakuttan. 'Gopi' gave me and my family crucial help and we remained friends until his untimely death in 2018. 'Kuttan' was my almost daily companion and guided me in the practicalities of contacting people and gathering data. Finally, I really appreciate how Ananya Jain and the editorial staff of Manohar transformed my manuscript skilfully into this beautiful book.

HANS SCHENK

CHAPTER 1

Introduction
Research on Alleppey

In May 1978 I paid my first visit to Alleppey. It could hardly be called a visit, just a stopover. An Indian friend and I travelled by car through Kerala from Trivandrum to Cochin along the coastal highway and we approached Alleppey from the South. (Figure 1.1) This Southern access to the town was not very spectacular. The road passes trough a sandy stretch of land with occasionally some paddy fields and many coconut trees. The countryside looked barren and not very inviting for a sojourn, and nor did the outskirts of the town. Huts and houses border the highway in gradually increasing numbers; rows of petty shops appear, some car repair sheds, and increasingly more people and vehicles. Then: a bus-stand, a row of taxis and many more people in between rows of two- and three-storeyed buildings. The highway narrows for a short while, and at the moment when one might think just to have passed the centre of a small district town, one meets the magic waterland of Alleppey, represented by its Commercial Canal as viewed from Iron Bridge (see Figure 1.2) We stopped beyond the bridge, and I took a few photographs: houses of red bricks and tiles; a canal green with weed and occasional blackish water; shallow colourless boats along the shores, some whitewashed with chalk.

Our trip through Kerala was intentional. My friend had accepted the participation in an Indo-Dutch research project which both my wife and I considered joining. Being in India I used the occasion to visit Kerala, see places, meet people and

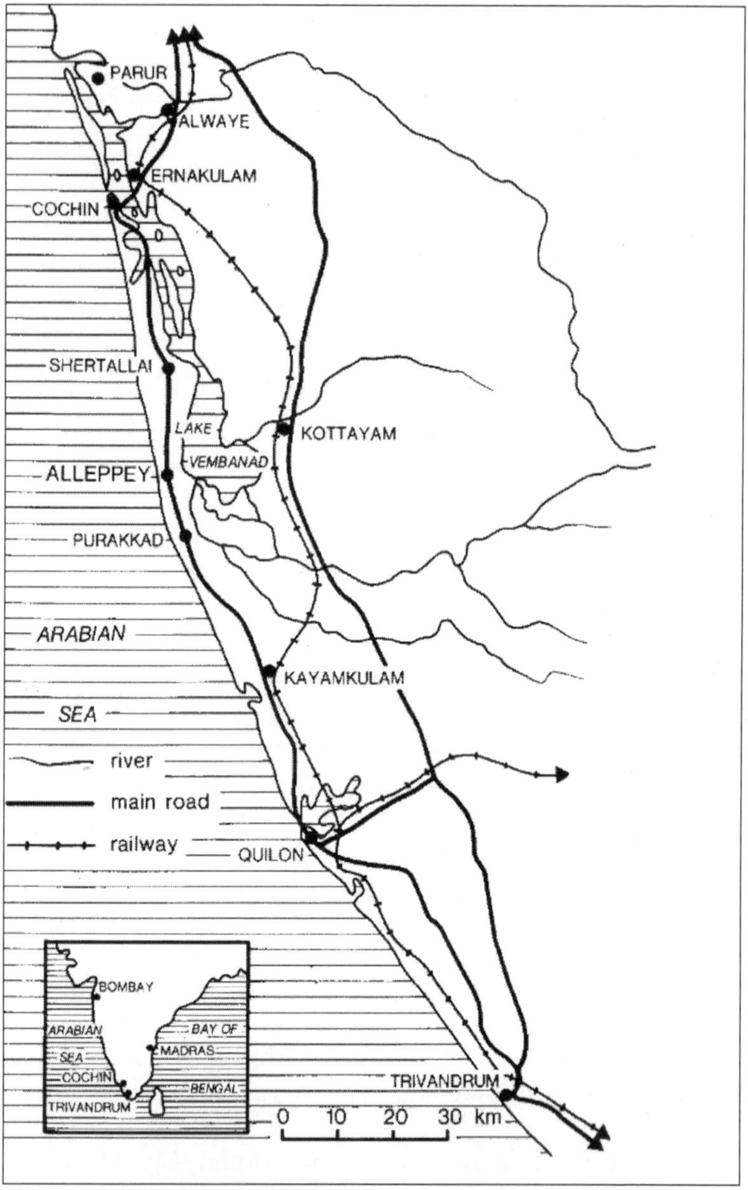

Figure 1.1: The location of Alleppey in South India. Sketchmap drawn by Hans Schenk/Jan ter Haar (University of Amsterdam).

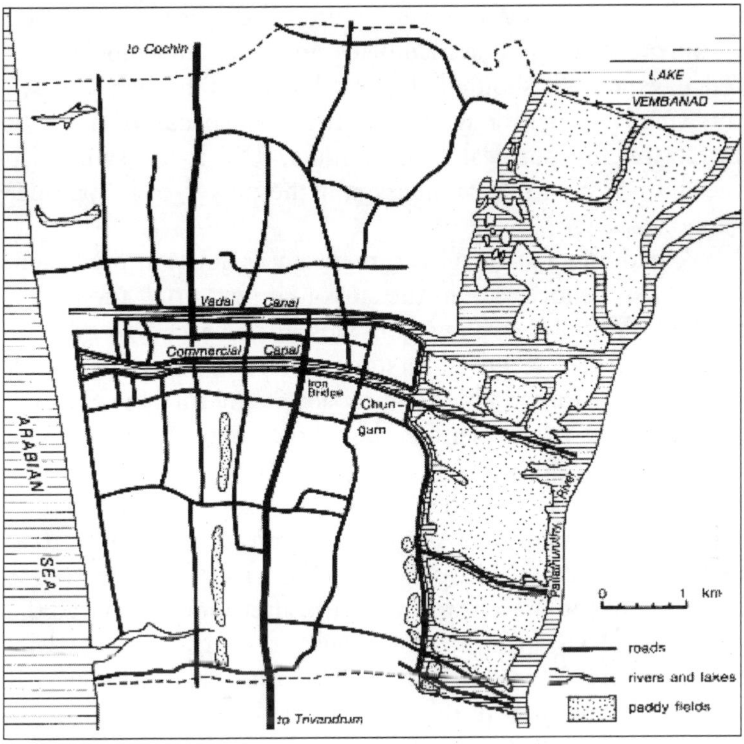

Figure 1.2: Sketchmap of Alleppey.
Sketchmap drawn by Hans Schenk/Jan ter Haar
(University of Amsterdam).

be shown around. The next day we had a few appointments in Alleppey—as it was a possible research location—and we drove back from Cochin together with some others. The next day I stood on the balcony of the district branch office of the State Bureau of Economics and Statistics. A pre-monsoon shower brought gentle rains and heavy, slow drops were transformed into innumerable circles in the water of Commercial Canal down below the office and just East of Iron Bridge. The banks of the canal, its houses and petty shops were soaked and contributed to the sad appearance of my view of the canal. On the opposite side a group of men and women appeared. The white *dhotis* of the men were soaked as well, but yet they were very white. The *saris* of the women colourful as ever. Some held black umbrellas, bot most waved red flags and all shouted slogans. How could I help but see this small event as a symbol of the very special position of Kerala on the political map of India? Did it not symbolize the 'leftist' state governments and the power of its popular support?

We had lunch at the government guest house at the beach. I went for a short walk in the surroundings, along the beach, to the lighthouse, to a few godowns, to the access to the pier stretching a few hundred meters into the Arabian Sea until a notice board forbade me to approach it any further. Not one human being was present in the whole area: nobody seemed to work in the godowns, nobody piled boats with cargo at the nearby end of Commercial Canal, nobody was on the pier. Did I see a dead part of Alleppey, remains of an outlived past, as the derelict buildings seemed to show: a superfluous appendix to the present town? In the afternoon we toured the town. We even saw a possible house to rent in case my wife and I should decide to stay and do research in Alleppey. It was on old mansion in the eastern part of the town, near the Chungam area where copra was dried, and coconut oil extracted.

Bewildering Alleppey! It looked to me like a forgotten fen peat colony in the north of the Netherlands in the 1950s. It looked to me like an unwanted monument to its past as a port, a port 'next to Bombay on the West coast', as it was said; a cradle of revolutionary perspectives for the Indian subcontinent, as it was said as well; a symbol of decay of entrepreneurial grandeur, both Indian and British. And yet, was there a town at all? Apart from the miserable, yet somewhat urban appearance of Commercial Canal and a very few streets and buildings, there was hardly a visible town. Houses hid behind compound walls and coconut trees. Missing were the crowded bazar-like areas and hectic traffic junctions which so obviously demonstrated urban life in many other towns and cities in India. Urban life here was rather invisible, and so were the inhabitants of Alleppey, some one hundred sixty-five thousand at that time.

Curiosity, or rather fascination, about the past and the present of Alleppey made me decide to prepare for the development of a design for the fieldwork-part of research in Alleppey in 1979.[1]

MAIN RESEARCH QUESTIONS, AND GIVEN ANSWERS IN THEMATIC-CHRONOLOGIES

This book on Alleppey is centred around a set of quite simple questions and attempts to answer these questions. In the first place, detailed answers are sought to be given to the question how Alleppey developed—for better or for worse, and functioned socio-economically and socio-spatially. Which stages in this development can be discerned and how have socio-economic and socio-spatial factors influenced and steered each other? How have these developments been experienced by the inhabitants of Alleppey or by certain stakeholders? Without framing possible answers to these and many more related research questions, I shall try to find answers by a detailed dive into Alleppey's past in the following parts, each consisting of a few chapters. These parts and chapters are for a great deal composed in thematic chronologies. That means, time and again will Alleppey's start, and its major landmarks come to the fore. However, they are each time embedded in the varying, particular context at stake: state formation, physical-geographical conditions, transport, available technology, economics, labour relations, perceptions, opinions, etc., etc.

The first part has been dedicated to the main political and economic factors which shaped Alleppey. In Chapter 2 it has been examined in which ways the formation of the erstwhile state of Travancore in the south-western corner of the South Asian subcontinent, and the growing power which this state could exercise in this region during the eighteenth century, influenced the birth of a port for the export of Travancore's spices at a hamlet named Alappuzha in 1762. This name corrupted soon, into Alleppey, together with the growth of the port and the emerging settlement. Travancore's declining power in relation to British supremacy through the East India Company and later the British Crown have been related to changes in Alleppey's economic activities. In Chapter 3 the relationship between economic development of the town and the dominant technical conditions which conditioned it, are discussed. It will be seen in which ways Alleppey was connected to modes of transport—both inland and overseas—and to prevailing transportation technologies. Chapter 2 ends at around year 1900, while developments after 1900 stand central in Chapter 4. This break is justified since about that time industrial activities gained momentum in Alleppey: the large-scale manufacturing of coir products: ropes, mats and matting, and the processing of other products provided by the coconut tree: copra and coconut oil. Large scale industrial production of coir products and overseas shipping of coir products have markedly added to the formerly dominant role of Alleppey as a trading and transport centre of pepper and other spices and have even overshadowed this role. At the same it became clear that the port could not meet anymore the trends in marine transport. In Chapter 4 the emphasis is on the nature of the industrial growth during several decades of the twentieth century and a rapid decline after Second World War. Also, here technical conditions (both industrial and for transport) have been related to these economic developments.

In Part Two social changes, spatial developments, the use and the meaning of local space and the local environment and its management come to the fore. The changes in the social structure of Alleppey have been examined in Chapter 5. Here, major social changes in Travancore in general, and in Alleppey in particular, have been related to economic developments. A wide variety of social changes can be seen. Mercantile communities were formed under the aegis of a strong state power during the eighteenth century. Missionaries and foreign entrepreneurs contributed to changing labour relations from a feudal society to an emerging class-pattern, in a long process that started during the nineteenth century and picked momentum in the twentieth century when labour unions and organizations of entrepreneurs opposed each other forcefully, though under conditions of economic decline. Chapter 6 is on the usage of the urban space of Alleppey related to local societal characteristics. It starts with the specific use of space related to Alleppey's start as a planned town in the eighteenth century, and deals with the ways in which site and societal characteristics interplayed in shaping the town during various stages of its history. Space and the ways it is used by the local society is not only factual, but it reflects societal forces and dominant cultures as well and can have symbolic meanings. In this chapter attention has also been given to the symbolic value to be attached to Alleppey's main structuring spatial element: its main water-transport artery: Commercial Canal. Space is also relevant in another way. It possesses environmental qualities, e.g. in the sense of public health standards. Local concern of public health stands central in Chapter 7, in which the related birth of urban local government comes to the fore.

Part Three is focused on local reactions to the changes that took place in the local society during the period of economic, social and political upheaval, roughly from the 1930s onwards and as experienced by local citizens. These changes were often dramatic and sudden, and moreover they have yielded many losers and probably few winners in the local society. This has created an atmosphere of bitterness and frustration in Alleppey and led to (orally and in the form of locally written sources) many analyses of what went wrong in the town, as well as 'what should be done' about it. This part consists of two chapters. In Chapter 8 many local interested people from diverse backgrounds gave opinions on selected broad topics of local interest, notably labour relations and the continuing concern about infrastructural deficiencies. In Chapter 9 the floor has been given to one single party: the formerly powerful Travancore Chamber of Commerce. The views of this entrepreneurial elite, through the annual speeches on world trade, the role of governments regarding entrepreneurs, labour and much more have been analysed in this chapter, till the Chamber lost its importance in the 1970s and its views on 'the world' were no longer recorded and made known on paper.

In a brief final epilogue, some of the main findings have been phrased in a nutshell and, while writing 'good-bye' to Alleppey, presented to the newly arisen (or re-arisen) settlement where it all started in 1762: Alappuzha.

NOTE

1. This research took place within the framework of an Indo-Dutch research project on Labour and Poverty in India and the Philippines, It was initiated at the erstwhile Department of South and Southeast Asian Studies at the University of Amsterdam, under general direction of O.D. Van den Muijzenberg and S. Devadas Pillai. My erstwhile Department of Urban Planning made my participation in 1979 in this project possible. The choice of Central Kerala was taken at project level, but Alleppey as the actual setting of research was chosen by my wife and me for various reasons. My wife found a large cluster of household servants in this town, which made her intended research on this occupational group attractive (see Schenk-Sandbergen, 1984; 1988). Apart from my initial fascination, the 'planned' origins of the town and the subsequent trade, industrial developments and wider societal processes of change that resulted from these origins, made Alleppey particularly attractive for the location of research. This book is a largely re-written version of my PhD dissertation: Views on Alleppey, University of Amsterdam/Royal Dutch Geographical Society, 1986.

PART ONE

CHANGING FUNCTIONS OF ALLEPPEY

CHAPTER 2

Formation and Deformation of Travancore State and its Foreign Trade Outlet

THE RISE OF TRAVANCORE AND THE BIRTH OF ITS POWER AND PRIDE: ALAPPUZHA/ALLEPPEY[1]

The start of the planned construction of Alappuzha as a state port for the export trade of the 'wealth of Travancore' in 1762 is an amazing phenomenon. It refers in the first place to state intervention in foreign trade, to the extent of active state involvement in the public works that were required to facilitate this trade. Activities undertaken on this scale were rare on the South Asian subcontinent during the eighteenth century. In the second place, the state involvement in foreign trade was meant to challenge the powers of foreign trading companies which tried to monopolize the overseas trade and transport of spices and other attractive items. Such companies became more and more successful in these aim during the eighteenth century, as has been well documented. Both aspects will be given more attention in the context of Travancore in this chapter.

A detailed account of the complex political and military situation of eighteenth-century Malabar, i.e. the south-western coastal area on the South Asian subcontinent goes beyond the scope of this analysis. It suffices here to mention that several allying and opposing powers—both local and foreign ones—played a role in a seemingly endless struggle for trade monopolies and territorial rights. In order to participate in the profitable business in pepper and other spices, a number of European sea-faring trade companies tried to develop their trading stations, 'factories', at many strategically situated locations. It was regularly attempted to expand the factories to mere walled and defensible settlements and subsequently to get some form of jurisdiction over small or larger regions, and thus over petty chieftains. Local rulers, sometimes rather independent, sometimes loosely or more tightly organized under the suzerainty of a major Raja, opposed the foreigners or sought their cooperation in order to oppose a neighbour or faraway enemy. One of the local powers during the 1700s was Travancore.

One major single force in the south-west of the sub-continent during the eighteenth century became the emerging state of Travancore.[2] This state was pushed by ambitious *raja*s: Raja Martanda Varma (1729-58) and Raja Rama Varma (1758-98), were assisted and guided by skilful ministers, of which Kesava Das (or Kesava Pillai) is generally considered as a brilliant administrator (Menon, 1967; Regional Records Survey Committee, 1970; Ouwerkerk, 1994).[3] Travancore extended during the eighteenth century gradually between the Indian Ocean and the hills of the Western Ghats, from Cape Comorin, the Southern tip of the subcontinent till Cranganore, 20 km north of Cochin. Beyond the control was the small but significant state of Cochin, protected by the Dutch from 1663 till 1795, and a number of minor trading posts, such Kayamkulam and Purakkad (in Dutch hands till the 1750s). The Travancore rulers were in those decades actively engaged in many public works, such as the opening of roads in the south of the state, the digging of canals which connected the elaborate system of natural waterways (the backwaters), the development of irrigation systems and the supply of drinking water (Menon, 1967: 265, 287). Meanwhile they brought the many petty rulers in the area under their command and laid the foundations for the development of Travancore as a strong state. Under these conditions of state involvement in Travancore's societal conditions was a port created, that became known as Alleppey, on the site of a village named Alappuzha.

The state saw it as a rewarding enterprise to have a state-controlled export outlet of its produce that was so much in demand abroad, and charged the State Commercial Department with the construction of this outlet. Hence, the state itself could and would participate in the lucrative trade of pepper and other species and of timber, which was at that time dominated by two foreign trading companies, the Dutch East Indies Company (VOC) and the British East India Company (EIC). The state endeavour of Travancore implied naturally a threat to foreign interests. The *raja*s of the state fought and won a number of military battles against the Dutch and finally broke Dutch power south of Cochin by the creation of Alleppey. Das Gupta has memorized this sequence of acts in the following words:

> Finally, Travancore challenged and broke the Dutch blockade of the coast at sea. This was done not by another naval battle but by the establishment of a new port at Alleppey a little to the south of Cochin, which the Dutch were forced to leave alone. All this took some fifty years to accomplish. In this half century the greatest single act in the business world of Malabar was the monopoly of Travancore. (1967: 33)

How can this successful attempt by Travancore to appear on the world trading map of the 1700s be explained? Two major factors must be mentioned in addition to the political and military strength of the state itself: (a) the struggle for supremacy among the European trading companies, and (b) the (alleged) military threats by other Indian powers to the eventual winner of the foreign power struggle, the EIC. These two factors worked sometimes together as shall be seen in the following brief overview:[4]

> The competition between European powers through their merchants' companies is a very complex issue that will not be dealt in general for the South Asian subcontinent, nor in its more detailed time- and place-bound details during the 1700s. Mukherjee may be right in his overall analysis of the EIC that the superior organization of the British trading company proved to be a decisive factor in gaining ultimate power on the subcontinent during the 1700s, but such a conclusion

cannot be drawn on a regional scale. The Dutch VOC was, even during the eighteenth century, a powerful force in the Southwest of the subcontinent, due to its possession of Cochin (till 1795), even though it lost influence in Travancore. The British held only a couple of minor factories along the Malabar coast. Besides, the French trading company, was during some decades around 1750, a competitor to both the EIC and the VOC, while afterwards it proved to be at least a nuisance to the British through its factory at Mahé, North of Cochin. Under these conditions of unstable mercantile dominance, much energy was spent in mutual out-manoeuvring. This increased the freedom of Travancore to expand its control over larger areas, over more people and over larger resources. This freedom was skilfully utilized in the process of the formation of the state: Travancore developed into a major regional power. The position of the state was also unchallenged between the 1750s and 1780s, as the then gradually most influential British considered the Travancorean power a minor problem, compared to the political and military expansion of Mysorean rulers towards Malabar. The presumed alliance between Mysore and French interests made the EIC focus its attention on the northern parts of present-day Kerala. After the British victory over these assumed rivals, the EIC decided to assume direct administrative power over this area, in order to safeguard its trading interests (Nightingale, 1970: 36-72).

The formation of Malabar district under the Bombay Presidency took place in 1792.

Hence, both the internal strength of Travancore, and the regional opportunities allowed for the creation of an outlet for its foreign trade. This started near the village Alappuzha in 1762, and by 1776 a port was fully functioning. However, the power of Travancore lasted for a brief time only. Though the state assisted even the British in fighting the Mysorean army in Malabar, the relations with the then powerful EIC deteriorated soon afterwards. Within a period of ten years, marked by a treaty in 1795 and a modified version of this treaty in 1805, Travancore was virtually transformed into a British dependency, protected by the EIC, for which it had to pay. The question whether an effective trade monopoly required political and military control as well, that was raised all over the subcontinent in the course of the eighteenth century, was also raised in its south-western corner. It was answered directly, as elsewhere in an affirmative way by the EIC. The strategic form of this affirmation was given in terms of 'indirect rule', unlike polities chosen by the EIC for Malabar district, where 'direct rule' was preferred.

The question why the British chose for indirect rule over Travancore to satisfy their interests has to be posed here since it mattered for the position of Travancore's foreign port, usually soon after its opening, becoming known as Alleppey. The answer must be found in the internal strength of the state. The northern parts of the Malabar cost were considered as unstable, in view of periodic attacks from the Indian state of Mysore. The periodic upheavals in this area did not exactly promote a 'trading climate' in which one single interest-group, the EIC could smoothly exercise its gained trading monopolies and fix the conditions of trade. This fact, and the urgency to expand the pepper trade to finance the almost bankrupt Bombay Presidency, required direct and stable British management, in the eyes of the company. The Malabar pepper made the Presidency survive! (Nightingale, 1970: 72). And indeed, as early as 1797 the EIC started a spice plantation in the then formed Malabar District (Menon, 1967: 336). In Travancore, according to the British, the existence of a strong and stable government did not require a direct rule. The administrative structure of the state proved to be helpful in controlling and increasing the cultivation of pepper and its sales thereafter. Hence, the EIC did not see it needy to engage in a relatively burdensome direct rule. The company assured, however, the control over crucial economic decisions. This control was in the first place institutionalized by the installation of a British Resident at the Travancore court. This Resident was a main factor in the control over state affairs, in particular regarding the duties to be paid to the British. This British position was in Travancore particularly rewarding to the company after 1810, when the Resident at that time, Colonel Munro, managed to manoeuvre himself into a fatherly position towards the then reigning *rani*.[5]

In the second place was the system of state monopolies in the trade of spices—called hill produce—that operated through state trading agents, brought under control by taking command of a crucial position in this trade. This position was taken by a nominated British Commercial Agent, in charge of the Commercial Department of Travancore. The Commercial Agents were stationed in Alleppey. In this way was the eminence of the port regarding foreign trade marked. At the same time the Commercial Agent was also appointed as superintendent of the local police and in charge of law and order in Alleppey.[6] It seems appropriate hence for all practical purposes to speak of 'British Alleppey' from the early 1800s onwards, in spite of the formal independence of the State of Travancore.

BRITISH POWER: FREE TRADE FOR TRAVANCORE

State monopolies in the export trade formed the backbone of the economy of Travancore. These monopolies were mainly related to hill-produce: spices like pepper and cardamom, but also salt, tobacco and opium. The monopoly system involved the activities of state trading agents who collected the produce at fixed prices and brought the export items from the 1770s onwards to Alleppey, where they were sold to the highest bidder. This system was vulnerable as state prices were lower than those at the 'black market' through smuggling. It did, moreover, not lead to an increasing supply of pepper and other export items through the Commercial Department. This state of affairs was used by the British Governor of Madras Presidency in 1855 to condemn the state monopoly system, for its promotion of smuggling and the endangering of public peace.[7] The condemnation was part of a letter to the then-reigning *raja* of Travancore and can be seen as an ultimatum to introduce several fiscal reforms in the state, or to undergo formal annexation by the British power—at that time still formally the EIC (RRSC-1, 1970: 117-19). The main reason for British action was, however, not the concern with smuggling that might endanger the 'public peace' which by the way benefitted the turnover of trade at the nearby port of British-Cochin. The concern focused rather on the insufficient incentives given for an intended increase of production of spices and the like, through the state monopoly system (see also Jeffrey, 1976: 63). The demand for pepper and other spices in an expanding worldwide market was the motive behind the proposal to introduce a liberalized economy in Travancore, in accordance with earlier similar developments in EIC-held parts of the subcontinent.[8] Free-trade and private enterprise were strongly advocated from Britain and these proved to be lucrative to British entrepreneurs. So, the British enforced the abolition of a couple of major state monopolies in Travancore. Pepper (from 1860 onwards) and tobacco (from 1863) were to be grown and/or traded freely, while an import and export duty of 15 per cent would partly compensate for the loss of income for the state. The British government finally subsidized the treasury of Travancore with an annual sum of 40,000 pounds to compensate for the remainder of the loss of state income. The state chronicler Aiya commented very positively on this measure:

> The interference of the State with the freedom of private production or distribution was reduced to a minimum and . . . the public had been given perfect liberty to import and export or deal in any article they like by simply undertaking to pay the Government fixed rates of import or export duties. (Aiya, 1906-III: 184)

An even stronger support for the imposition of free-trade was given by the Regional Records Survey Committee (RRSC), which, after acknowledging the benefits of free-trade, asked for attention to the persisting salt monopoly. (RRSC-1, 1970: 60). The imposition of free trade got another impetus when, in 1865, Travancore joined the British Indian Free Trade Zone. Shortly afterwards, in 1866, the British Crown, satisfied with the behaviour of the *raja* of Travancore, upgraded his title to *maharaja* (Aiya, 1906-I: 553).

The imposition of free trade symbolises British power against a powerless state on the subcontinent. But it did, after all, not much harm to the state treasury. The losses to state income after the reduction of state income due to the collection of duties, appears to have been compensated by the general expansion of the value of foreign trade since the 1860s. (Jeffrey, 1976: 96-8). This expansion can at least be partly explained by the advent of a new generation of merchants from abroad, penetrating Travancore from the 1860s onwards. The economic gains seem also to have been dominant as well, at least for a small commercial elite. Thus, in the short term, the interests of the State of Travancore and those of (mostly British) entrepreneurs coincided sufficiently as the increase of trade brought wealth to the latter and income from duties to the former. On the other hand, however, Travancore lost what was left of its grip on the export trade of the state, and this proved to be a major loss as shall be seen later in this chapter. Finally, the main winners were the entrepreneurs themselves, and among them the foreign ones—mainly Englishmen and Scotsmen who benefited the most. Henceforth they could operate without interference on the sites of production in Travancore, while they monopolized the consumers' markets elsewhere in the world. To some extent it can be said that the head office of Travancore's foreign trade was removed from Alleppey—from the Commercial Department of the state—to the city of London.

BRITISH POWER: THE HARBOUR OF COCHIN

The next major event marking the dominance by British India over Travancore occurred when the provincial government of Madras decided to build a modern deep-water harbour at British Cochin, 60 km north of Alleppey. This decision was finally taken in the early 1920s and it took fifteen years to be implemented. This endeavour was opposed by many: by entrepreneurs in Alleppey and elsewhere; by some shippers in Cochin who had specialized in lighter traffic to the roadstead of Cochin in the Arabian Sea; by railroad authorities who were afraid to lose income as rail routes were shortened and who moreover had to share profits with the state of Cochin; by traders even as far as Bombay and Madras. On the other hand, promotors were mainly found among the British Indian Navy and the British Admiralty who thought of employing the deep-water harbour as a navy shelter in times of war (Bristow, 1959: 179-88; Meile, 1939). The construction of the harbour can be seen as a public undertaking on a scale that could not be realized by private developers with private funds. The Alleppey merchants were able to deal with the scale of the improvements of 'their' port during the nineteenth-century, as shall be seen in the next chapter, but there was no chance for them to compete with this operation undertaken by state intervention with public funds.

State intervention is a composite term to describe the co-operation of relevant authorities in the development of the harbour. Beside Madras Province (and at a later stage the Imperial British-India government in New Delhi), the states of Cochin and Travancore co-financed 'Cochin'.

The motives of the State of Cochin are clearly understandable: the state was to attract additional trade and transport and could draw the revenues of it. Besides, it could be expected that the harbour would attract other economic activities. Cochin did not, moreover have many options: British-Indian pressures were strong enough as the project required Cochin's participation since a part of its territory was involved. But Travancore was in a different position.

Travancore was formally an outsider in the project, and in theory it could have ignored the construction of Cochin's harbour. In practice, however, the development of Cochin would naturally divert even more traffic from Alleppey and elsewhere in the state than was already going on since the late 1800s and early 1900s. Hence, Travancore had also little to choose anymore. Whereas Travancore was able in 1762 to challenge foreign trade dominance, it had lost its grip on the pattern of foreign trade since the imposition of free trade in the 1860s and could not do without the remaining trade duties. The state was also unable to provide a viable alternative within Travancore: not even Alleppey could become such a viable alternative option as will also become clear later in this study. Thus, the only way open in the perception of the Travancore administration, was to participate in Cochin's development and participate in its expected returns as well.

In view of the list of opposing parties to the development of Cochin's harbour, and in view of the meagre list of public defendants, it is at first sight hard to understand why Madras province proposed and decided to go ahead with the ambitious project at all. The only plausible explanation is in terms of the mentioned merits of the harbour as a naval station for the British Indian navy. From the beginning of the decision-making process, it was decided by the navy and the British Admiralty that a naval and air base should be part of the military infrastructure of British India. Apparently, this wish had been a long-standing one (of course, pertaining to a naval station only). Nightingale mentions that the British were directly, after as far back as 1789, considering making Cochin into: 'a first-class military station' at the cost of Bombay (1970: 48). This simple pressure outbalanced all other doubts, hesi-tations, and objections and was decisive. However, Bristow remarked with some amazement that the Navy and the Admiralty did not intend and did not contribute one single rupee or pound sterling towards the undertaking. (Bristow, 1959: 186).

The port of Alleppey, and also other ports in the Malabar district saw their share in the overseas trade diminished due to the opening of Cochin's modern harbour in the 1930s. But even long before this harbour became accessible to modern steamers, much trade and transport had already shifted to Cochin, as will be seen in the following chapter. Neither Travancore state, nor merchants' lobbies in Alleppey could influence the events that affected the state, the entrepreneurs and many others. The deformation of Travancore state was in full swing from the late 1800s onwards and got an extra impetus by the British Indian armed forces.

ALLEPPEY: FROM THE MAJOR PORT OF TRAVANCORE TO A MINOR PORT OF INDIA

The final stage in the process of deformation of Travancore, was of course the merger of the state with the independent Indian Union in 1949. An independent Travancore was envisaged for a short while by its administration in the years following India's independence in 1947. However, this plan proved to be unrealistic and was challenged by popular demand to join India, which happened in 1949. From being the major port of Travancore between 1762 and 1949 Alleppey became overnight a minor one in India. Its position in India will be examined in some more detail in subsequent chapters (see the Chapters 8 and 9), but it is relevant to state already here that since 1949 decisions regarding the port were made in faraway New Delhi, which has certainly contributed to the neglect of Alleppey's interests.

Mention should also be made at this point of Alleppey's position in a wider worldwide structure of economic and political power. Alleppey's trade (and later its industries—processing of coir into mats and matting, see Chapter 3) functioned largely as an 'out-station' of British entrepreneurial interests between the 1860s and the late 1940s. This meant for example that even though the United States started to restrict the import of especially coir goods around 1900, the products of the then quickly expanding coir industry in Alleppey found their way easily to Britain, its Commonwealth and to a few European countries. After the Second World War and India's Independence many changes took place in this respect. One change was the weakened possibility to sell Travancorean and Indian goods. Coir products and other goods were taxed increasingly, not only for leaving India, but also on entering the principal consumer markets in Western Europe and elsewhere. British companies in Alleppey became

'Indianized' and lost in due course the privileged access to London which the British merchants so easily had. It should be added that a range of other factors also played a role in the course of industrial development of Alleppey, as will be seen in subsequent chapters. A more balanced picture of the changed position of Alleppey can only be drawn in a much later stage in this study.

CONCLUDING REMARKS

It can be said, when summarizing this chapter, that Alleppey was an exponent of a powerful regional political unit on the subcontinent during a very limited period. It lasted from the inception of the port in 1762 till around 1800, when Travancore's power was initially curtailed by the EIC; further around 1860 when free-trade was imposed on the state and its foreign trade; and finally from the 1930s onwards when a far superior harbour very nearby was opened for the export produce of Travancore.

However, despite this picture of a weakened state of Travancore, Alleppey fared well! At last, till the Second World War, as shall be seen in the next two chapters. Can one then assume that the position of Travancore did not matter very much to Alleppey, after the end of the initial start under state guidance? Did not the economic position of the town and its port rely more on foreign (British) developments than on those in Travancore since about 1800? Or, to say the least, was the step by step weakened position of Travancore outweighed by other factors which affected the local society and the local economy in a positive way? The following chapters deal with such questions.

NOTES

1. It is historically correct to write about the mere fishing village Alappuzha as the origin of a trade outlet in Travancore in the eighteenth century. In the course of the eighteenth century this name

was corrupted into Alleppey. This name became the name of the settlement till 2012, when Alappuzha formally regained its original name, though 'Alleppey' remains widely used.

2. Travancore is the Anglicized version of Thiruvithakoor. The state formed with Cochin (Kochi) and British ruled Malabar in 1956 in the Indian state of Kerala.
3. Kesava Das is generally known as Raja Kesava Das. He was the chief (*diwan*) of Travancore from 1788 onwards, and before that time in charge of the Commercial Department of the state. Lord Wellesly, governor-general of the British EIC at Calcutta gave him the title of *raja*.
4. Ramkrishna Mukerjee's analysis of the EIC forms an outstanding general overview (1974), while for more limited periods and for more limited regions, the studies of among others Pamela Nightingale on the supremacy over the 'coast of Malabar' (1970), and that of Rajendran on the same topic should be mentioned (1979), together with the works of Poonen on the VOC at the Malabar coast (1948, 1978).
5. The *rani* spoke the following words in her inaugural address: 'I cannot do better than to place myself under the guidance and support of the Honourable East India Company whose bosom has been an asylum for the protection of an infant like Travancore since the time Sree Padmanabha Swamy had effected an alliance with a respectable Company of the European nation. To you, Colonel I entrust everything connected with my country and from this day I look upon you as my elder brother' (RRSC: 40).
6. See Chapter 6 for a few more details.
7. The Governor of Madras Presidency was the next to the highest level of authority of the EIC. (Three years later, in 1858 British Crown took over the EIC and its possessions and interests, other assets, and liabilities transferred to the British Crown.)
8. The trade monopoly of the EIC ended in 1833.

CHAPTER 3

Natural Conditions, Technical Progress, and Economic Growth in Alleppey, 1762-1900

THE SITE OF ALLEPPEY: OPTIMIZATION OF PHYSICAL GEOGRAPHICAL CONDITIONS UNDER PREVAILING MODES OF TRANSPORT

When in the mid-1700s the Government of Travancore decided to take an active part in the profitable overseas trade of its spices, timber and other 'produce of the coast of Malabar', the actual implementation of this decision implied the selection of a site for a port town. This selection was largely governed by physical-geographical considerations and prevailing modes of inland transport. These two decisive factors will be discussed in the first part of this chapter. In subsequent parts takes technical progress with regard to the functioning of this seaport in a central position.

A to-be-developed port town had to be based on inland water transport under the prevailing conditions of eighteenth-century Travancore. Overland means of transportation of cargo hardly existed. The earliest well-known survey of the means of communication in the state, by Ward & Connor, mentions only very few roads, accessible to 'troops moving with heavy artillery' and some more footpaths and tracks, usable for donkeys, bullocks and coolie-porterage.[1] The main reason for the absence of overland roads lies in the physical-geographical conditions of large parts of the state, in particular in the north-west. In this area dominates a culmination of the interplay of sea, rivers, and alluvial deposits (see Figure 3.1).

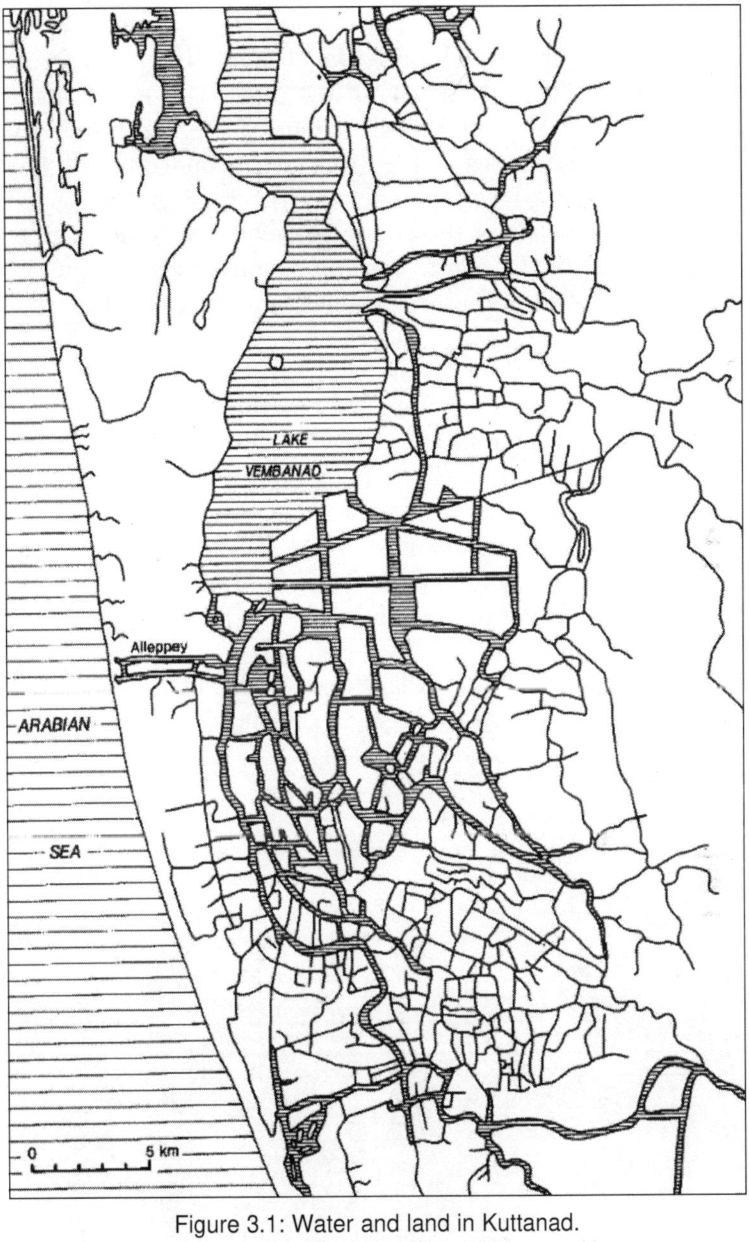

Figure 3.1: Water and land in Kuttanad.
Sketchmap drawn by Hans Schenk/Jan ter Haar
(University of Amsterdam).

The north-west is in fact a huge lagoon. Going from West to East, the Western stretch of Travancore consists of a narrow sandy coastal strip, dotted with low dunes and occasionally broken by sea inlets and small streams. The elevations can hardly be called dunes as they do not rise more than a few meters above sea level and the tiny fishermen's huts which are scattered all along the coast are frequently washed away by the waves of the south-west monsoon winds, in spite of incidental protection in the form of low stone dykes here and there.

The dune belt is only a few kilometres wide and gradually passes into a low-lying zone of marshy and peaty lands, intersected by a myriad of waterways. This area culminates in north-west Travancore in the complex network of rivers and rivulets, lakes, islands, and sea inlets, which is called the Kayals—or Backwaters (Figure 3.2). The Backwaters cover an area of about 160 km north to south, from Cranganore to Quilon (now Kollam), and up to 30 km from west to east.

Figure 3.2: The Backwaters (Photograph by Hans Schenk).

The backwaters can be considered as an enormous intermediate basin between the numerous rivers flowing westwards from the hills of the Western Ghats towards the Arabian Sea. Fresh water is brought to the backwaters by the rivers and the monsoon rains, while salt water is added at high tides, mainly through two major sea inlets, one in the south not far from Quilon, and another more to the north nearby Cochin.[2] The central part of the backwaters is dominated by a sizeable stretch of open water (Vembanad Lake), covering an area of 60 km north to south. More to the south are the river outlets into the lake increasingly mixed with pieces of land—submerged from time to time.

This land- and waterscape is somewhat comparable with conditions in the western parts of the Netherlands, before the era of reclaiming the many inland lakes and waters, from the late Middle Ages onwards. This comparison with 'Holland' is also valid in recent time. Parts of the Kuttanad area have been bunded, while adjoining parts of Vembanad Lake have been reclaimed from water and transformed into polders. This scheme is known as the 'Holland-scheme' (see also, Government of Kerala, 1974). The comparison with 'Holland' was apparently also made already in 1664 by the Dutch captain of the VOC, who toured the area. In the Alleppey District Gazetteer (Government of Kerala, 1975: 64) the following lines have been written: 'Nieuhoff proceeded to Kudumalur by boat along the lakes of Kuttanad which evoked in his mind nostalgic memories of his own native land'.

The rivers feeding Vembanad Lake flow directly south of the lake through Kuttanad, and then converge more or less at the south-western corner of the lake, at a site where the sandy coastal strip that makes for the western border of the backwaters is rather narrow: some 5 km wide. This location was chosen for the new port of Travancore (see Figure 3.1). Not only could inland water transport function in an optimal way when it was directed to the site of the future Alleppey, there was another asset in the region as well. In the absence of real harbour facilities along Travancore's coast, overseas shipping had to take place at the roadstead, from lighters into sea-going vessels. Off the coast at the site designated to become the new port were the roadstead protected against rough seas by a mud bank, the Chakara, which provided for a relatively safe anchorage and place for transhipment, even during monsoon.[3]

The site to build the port was thus convenient enough given prevailing transport facilities and possibilities and given natural conditions. The broad or narrow, straight or crooked, deep or shallow inland waterways could be plied by large and small boats (*vellam*) and canoes which could bring the precious cargo—pepper, other spices, timber, etc.—downstream with the help of small sails or by human power. The British naval engineer Robert Bristow who occasionally sailed the backwaters during the 1920s and 1930s, writes at length to depict inland boat traffic:

> The backwater craft were called wallum (or vellams). There were first, second and third-class wallums, according to size and quality of construction. They had a spirally curved finish to the bow and stern, or some other attempt at a terminal feature. Like the lighters, the bow and stern were the same, and the boats travelled with equal facility in either direction. As protection for cargo, they had a scientific contraption of palm leaf and split bamboo which arched from side to side as the beam width narrowed fore and aft from the centre. In this centre, for the convenience of the crew, there was a movable section overlapping the others. It was a most efficient and adaptable form of construction. Heavy loads of five ton or more could be carried, and the smaller craft, it seemed, could almost navigate the ditches of the countryside. It was sailed, or poled, or rowed; or in very shallow water, pushed, the crew jumping overboard for the purpose. It provided the cheapest form of transport in the world, or at any rate one of the cheapest, which during the nineteenth century, was stated to have cost about the equivalent of one farthing per ton per mile. Its use dated back to prehistoric times. (1959: 52-3)

Apart from the mentioned site assets the area was hardly inviting to settle. Both the sandy coastal strip and the backwater complex seem to have been a mere tropical jungle, inhabited mainly by monkeys, jackals and crocodiles, according to several accounts of the early history of the area (Menon, 1967: 279; Government of Kerala, 1975: 87). Aiya writes about a water basin adjoining Alleppey to the East that it was infested by alligators of enormous size (1906).

The construction of the port started to take shape around the year 1762 under the direction of the Government of Travancore. Basically, its lay-out was simple and logical. Besides the clearance of a section of the jungle a canal was dug, or rather extended from an existing water course, across the dunes, close to the beach and the Arabian Sea. A tiny hamlet at the eastern side of this canal, named Alappuzha, gave its name to the new port town, but, as I wrote above, this name was subsequently corrupted by the British into its Anglicized form: Alleppey.[4] The canal—later named Commercial Canal—was to be the lifeline of the 'new town' of Travancore (Figure 3.3). Along its banks the Government Trading Office and a number of godowns were built. Due to the absence of an indigenous foreign-trading tradition,

Figure 3.3: Commercial Canal (Photograph by Hans Schenk).

merchants from elsewhere in the subcontinent were invited by the Travancore government to come, trade, and stay in Alleppey (see further in Chapter 5).

How Alleppey got started is known in some detail,[5] but much less is known about its subsequent history till the mid-1800s. Though major changes took place after 1800 with regard to the control over the export trade of the state (as described in Chapter 2) and although changes were initiated in its social structure (as will be seen in Chapter 5), the technical conditions which gave rise to the birth of the town did not change in any considerable way between 1762 and—say—1850. Neither did its *raison-d'être* change: the overseas export of the 'wealth of Travancore'. Inland water transport and the roadstead remained dominant in the transportation scene. It may be assumed that a gradual expansion of the volume of trade and transport took place, as during the first half of the nineteenth century a second canal, Vadai Canal, parallel to Commercial Canal was dug. More commercial space was apparently needed to relieve overcrowding of Commercial Canal and/or its banks (Jeffrey, 1976: 32). In an internal report from the Swiss trading company Volkart Brothers, which settled along the coast of Malabar in 1860, this (approximate) period been recalled in the following words:

> Alleppey counted in these days less than 15,000 inhabitants . . . with jungle strewn over the entire area. Communication facilities by road were sparse, but water transport was fairly well developed with two canals connecting the port and the backwater. (Quoted from Unnithan, 1970: 10)

NEW TECHNICAL DEVELOPMENTS, NEW OPPORTUNITIES

The 1860s marked a new phase in the history of Alleppey. Rapid changes in the infrastructural facilities of the port took place, more or less simultaneously with technical developments in the town. Besides, the nature of the local economy started to change. The rapid penetration of European entrepreneurs into Travancore and Alleppey under the new regime of free trade in the state was an attempt to tap the existing natural resources, the 'wealth of Travancore' in a more exhaustive way, and an impetus to develop and tap novel resources of wealth.

New Technical Developments

First, a brief overview will be given of major technical innovations regarding the economic life of Alleppey, and especially pertaining to its trade and transport, which took place during the second half of the nineteenth century. The list of innovations starts with the opening in Alleppey in 1857 of the first modern post office; the first in Travancore. The British postal system was introduced to the state and the town and was added to the traditional *anchal* postal system. This event symbolizes the felt need to establish this form of institutionalized communication with the outside world. Alleppey was a forerunner in Travancore as it took six to eight years before such Western postal facilities were set up in other major urban places in Travancore, including its capital city Trivandrum (Aiya, 1906-II: 243). A few years later, in 1860, began the construction of a lighthouse. It took two years to complete this sizeable undertaking in the context of a small town. The costs of construction (£1667; sic, HS) were covered by port-dues imposed on the shipping traffic by the Commercial Department of the state (Aiya, 1906-I: 535; RAT 1865-6: 37). In 1863 the first telegraph office in Travancore was opened in Alleppey, connecting the port with British Cochin. Later on, the telegraph line was extended southward to Tuticorin.

In the administrative year 1871-2 a 'rough wooden pier' was built at the beach, in order to facilitate the loading and unloading of the lighters, by the Commercial Department. This pier did not last long unfortunately. It was reported to be out of order after a few years but put in working condition again a year later (RAT 1871-2: 48; RAT 1874-5: 59; and RAT 1875-6: 69 respectively). A cyclone destroyed the pier again in 1879, and subsequently a temporary jetty was built (RAT 1878-9: 110). A more permanent solution was reached with the start of the building of an 'iron screw pier' in 1880 (RAT 1880-1: 58) which was still standing at the turn of the century and renewed only in 1907. However, due to a recession of the sea it was extended in 1892-3 and provided with a railway and cranes (RAT 1892-3: 104; and Pillai, 1940: 193, respectively). Inside the town area the most significant innovation of the system of transportation was the digging of a small canal connecting the two main east-west running canals: Commercial Canal and Vadai Canal. It was suggested to dig this canal in the late 1870s and was probably ready in 1887 (RAT 1886-7: 104). At the same time the Vadai Canal was deepened and made more suitable for inland water transport.

This list of major innovations shows the type of technical improvements that were considered important to the port and the town. In retrospect they may not look impressive, but they were apparently sufficient for the demand of transport in the nineteenth century. In the report of the 1901 Census of India the port was described in the following way:

> (Alleppey) . . . commands a fine harbour affording safe anchorage for the greater part of the year. . . . It affords a convenient depot for the storage and disposal of hill produce. (Census of India 1901, vol. XXVI, part 1, 1903: 23)

Yet, even this modest list of technical innovations led the port and its supporting infrastructural facilities close to its limits to modernize, as shall be seen in a later part of this chapter. Already during the 1890s the Government of Travancore decided not to develop Alleppey's port any further, but to foster the outgrowth of the competing port of Cochin, beyond the state's territory.

New Institutions

Technical developments that took place between about 1850 and 1900 were apparently matched by institutional reforms.

These reforms were of various kinds: removal of trade barriers, regulation of port facilities and the separation of the port as an institutional entity from the urban place which gradually developed and expanded around it. (see also Chapters 5 and 6). As has been seen in the preceding chapter, the abolition of state control over the major products of Travancore's export trade had largely been dictated by political power exercised from outside the state. Free trade, however, turned out to be an impetus for its economic growth, as it attracted new entrepreneurs from abroad who had access to new and to expanding foreign consumers' markets. Since about 1860 foreign 'merchants' adventurers', a name they sometimes proudly brandished, settled in Alleppey (Langley, n.d.). Their presence demanded at least 'public rules and regulations' regarding the use of the facilities offered by the port authority, the Commercial Department. Before free trade was imposed, such rules and regulations might have been in existence, but these should be seen as an internal affair of the Commercial Department. Since the 1860s steps were undertaken to distinguish between 'port' and 'citizens using it'. Also in another way steps were taken leading to a separation between the port and the town of Alleppey and its citizens. Until probably the 1890s the Commercial Agent was responsible both for the management of the port and in charge of civil duties, such as the maintenance of law and order, and public health care. With the introduction of local government in Travancore, through installed Town Improvement Committees in 1894-5, were 'urban requirements' distinguished from those of the port, and funds to look after these requirements came from different sources. In Chapter 7 the start and further functioning of local government in Alleppey will be discussed in some detail.

New Dimensions in Shipping

> Transport is often given a dull factual treatment.
>
> (Kemp, 178: 172)

It is now opportune to look at the counterpart of technical innovations and emerging new institutions: transport itself. There is only scattered information about it but the picture is clear enough. In short, larger and increasingly steam-powered ships plied at the port of Alleppey (or rather its roadstead), collecting more cargo, and also starting to delivering goods.[6] In the Report of the Administration of Travancore for the administrative year 1865-6 it was stated that: '1 steamer, 79 ships, 10 barks, 38 brigs, 23 schooners and a number of smaller vessels' called at the port, in all having a tonnage of 74,028 (RAT, 1865-6: 37). Such detailed information about the number and the types of ships calling at Alleppey is only rarely available for other years. Only during eight consecutive years in the 1870s was a distinction in types of ships (steamers, square rigged vessels and small, coastal craft) made and published. The statistics for these years show a rapid increase in the number of steamers, from around fifty in the early 1870s to over hundred at the end of the decade. The tonnage of the ships that called at the roadstead increased in total, mainly due to the increased number of ever bigger steamers. The average steamer doubled its loading capacity in only five years: from 544 tons in 1873-4 to 1,173 tons five years later. The statistics of the 1870s show a widening gap as well between the traditional overseas and coastal transport by sailing vessels on the one hand and the new steamships on the other hand (see for details: Appendix, Table 1).

Not much detailed information is available for the 1880s and 1890s, but it seems that the picture that appeared from the 1870s continued, though with some ups and downs. The total tonnage of ships calling at the port of Alleppey rose steadily: from around 70,000 tons in the early 1870s, via 150,000 in the late 1870s, to over 250,000 tons in the late 1880s and 1890s. There is only one possible conclusion to draw from these statistics: Alleppey's trade increased. This conclusion was already drawn in 1872 (RAT 1871-2: 49), and seemed valid for the following decades as well.

Trade: Traditional and New Products

Now the question arises what was actually traded, and transported to and especially from Alleppey. Traditionally a major item among the exports from the port was spices, especially pepper. After all the port was started mainly for these products. According to the duties collected from the export trade from Travancore, either overland, by sea or across the backwaters to Cochin, a quarter consisted in the middle of the 1860s of duties from pepper exports (RAT 1865-6: 33). Thirty years later, however, the share of pepper in the exports from Travancore was only 9 per cent (RAT 1896-7: 94). This does not mean that the volume of the pepper exports diminished structurally during this period,[7] but it merely means that a more sizeable share of the exports consisted of other items. In addition to pepper and other spices there was the trade in dried ginger, jaggery, timber, tea, coffee and a number of other items. However, by far the most important items during the second half of the nineteenth century, became the products of the coconut tree: copra, coconut oil and coir products. These products formed about 50 per cent of the export value of the export trade from Travancore around 1900. And thus, as Prakash writes: '. . . vast areas of waste lands, lands in riverbanks, backwaters, valleys, hill slopes etc. were brought under coconut cultivation' (2018: 9-10). Their growing importance is related to a new type of innovation brought to Alleppey: the introduction and subsequent implementation of industrial technology.

Emerging Industrial Technology

The major event to account for the larger share of the products of the coconut tree in the exports from Alleppey, was the weaving of coconut mats from corn yarn with the help of machines. Woven products of coir yarn came in addition to a long-standing modest export of coir yarn and coir rope. The introduction of woven items, named 'mats & matting' became of enormous importance for the economy of Alleppey. It brought innovative technology to the town, implemented in new industrial enterprises. It brought employment for many thousands of men and women in the town and its surrounding and it gave a strong impetus to a new style of labour relations during the 1900s.

The manufacturing of coir mats and matting brought the fabrication of end coir products to the town in 1859, when James Darragh, an American of Irish descent, started his business in Alleppey. Before that year, mat weaving took place on a modest scale in the United States and in Europe only. The availability of raw material—the locally and regionally produced yarn from the coconut fibre—brought Darragh to Alleppey.[8] The entrepreneurial activities in this new industrial sector in the decades following 1859 were very much of a frontier type, as Langly (n.d.) shows. Entrepreneurs came and went, some made fortunes, while others failed. Companies merged and split. However, the technical dimension of industrial enterprise took root in Alleppey, though its most visible dimension, 'machinery', came only gradually to the town. In the Administrative Report of Travancore for the year 1871-2, it is mentioned that: 'More steam machinery is being brought into use for the manufacturing of coir matting and for expressing oil' (RAT, 1871-2: 49). The mentioning of expressing oil with machine-power is the first available reference about the crushing of copra into coconut oil by steam machine. According to Aiya, this attempt of using machines to crush copra failed at that time, while a more successful steam-powered oil mill started to function around the turn of the century (Aiya, 1906-II: 19). All together, and according to Aiya, Alleppey counted around the year 1900, five factories, of which three were steam powered (1906-II: 295). These figures indicate that the modern industrialization of Alleppey during several decades after 1859 should not be overestimated. Alleppey's first and still major manufacturing (and trading) firm, James Darragh's, consisted—probably in the year 1889—of the following items:

This in those days consisted of a small Factory where the manufacture of Coir Mattings principally for the American market was carried, a Bailing Press and the necessary sorting sheds for the preparation of the yarn, a Bleaching shed for the preparation of Coffee and the necessary godowns. . . . At the time of Mr. Darragh's departure for Home very few mats were being made and a great many of the buildings were only of a Cutcha construction that is to say, made of timber posts with sides and roofs of bamboo with thatch (coconut leaves plaited). (Davey, n.d.: 8)

INFRASTRUCTURAL AND OTHER INNOVATIONS IN TRAVANCORE: THREATS TO ALLEPPEY

Though Alleppey could profit in the short term from technical innovations—benefitting its trade and transport, and to a lesser extent its newly-developed industrial economy—elsewhere in Travancore too, changes took place. Some of these changes benefited the town, but other ones posed serious challenges to its economy. A brief overview will give an impression of the mood of free trade and development along capitalist lines that started in the middle of the nineteenth century and left imprints on the local society of Alleppey. Travancore witnessed a strong commercialization of its agricultural activities during the second half of the nineteenth century. This culminated in an emerging plantation economy that started in 1855 (Lemercinier, 1983: 224-6). Already in the 1860s many acres of land in Travancore were sold to European planters. Not less than 86,000 acres (34,800 ha) to a few planters, according to Ibrahim (1878: 38).[9] Namboodiripad related this process of the commercialisation of agriculture to food scarcities (famines occurred in 1860 and in 1870), and to rice imports since about 1870. He writes: 'Only the barest minimum of food was produced for the purpose of local consumption.' (1967: 85). On the other hand, the cultivated area increased considerably from about the year 1850 onwards, due to the sale of state-owned wastelands to cultivators, followed by a spurt in land reclamation, notably in the Backwaters region (Varghese, 1970: 64-5, 119). From the early 1900s onwards, large-scale backwater-reclamations were undertaken on capitalist lines organized by Christians and financed by banks (Varghese, o.c.: 119-20). However, since no data exist for the period prior to 1920 with regard the use of land in terms of food- and cash-crops, it is difficult to gauge the impact of the enlarged cultivated area.[10] Whereas the commercialized agriculture might have benefitted Alleppey's trade and transport activities, some concerns about its future could be observed as well by the end of the nineteenth century. But seeds were sown for its industrial growth, and technical support for the promotion of trade and transport was in full bloom during the second half of the nineteenth century, as was mentioned earlier in this chapter. But one might even state that the blossoming was already fading away, while signs of decay became visible. What basically happened regarding this signalled decay, was that—again from the 1860s onwards—the transportation system on which Alleppey was based (water transport) began to be replaced by a more modern system.

Travancore had in the 1860s one single road accessible to wheeled traffic. This road linked the capital city Trivandrum to southern places in Madras Province, east of Travancore. In that decade started an ambitious road-construction programme, 'aimed largely at the exploitation of the trade and agricultural potential of the state' (Ibrahim, 1978: 38; see also Jeffrey, 1976: 90-6). This programme resulted in an impressive increase of road mileage, from 52 in 1860 to 900 in 1880 and 3,000 in 1900. A major artery that was negatively relevant for Alleppey was the constructed 'Main Central Road' (even now called 'MC Road'), connecting Trivandrum in the south with a number of smaller population centres in the centre and the north of the state. This road runs east of the backwater-system and lies about 20 to 30 km east of the coast in the so-called 'Midland' area. On the western side of Travancore no such a north-south running coastal trunk road was planned for the time being. MC Road served as the major—actually the only—trunk road in the state. It appeared to function in an excellent way as an artery carrying the 'hill-produce' (spices, coffee, tea, rubber after 1900) brought to it by minor feeder roads, to convenient sea outlets. Such an outlet was mainly found at Ernakulam-Cochin, in neighbouring Cochin State. As no road access was made to Alleppey, the modern transport system tended to isolate the town from a sizeable part of its hinterlands: the hills and the midlands. For the time being it was a tendency only, as water transport still far outweighed any other mode of transport in the northern regions of Travancore. And to this should be added that some improvements were even made in the system of waterways. But the early 1900s saw a further threat to the inland water-transport by the introduction of railways in south-west India. In 1902 Ernakulam—bordering Cochin—was connected to the network of the Madras and Southern Mahratta railways, eventually connecting this town with Madras (Central Station). Moreover, Quilon (now Kollam), 80 km south of Alleppey became in 1904 the terminus of the Southern Indian Railways, which connected this place with a minor port eventually also with Madras (Egmore Station).[11] Figure 3.4 shows schematically how new overland transportation routes

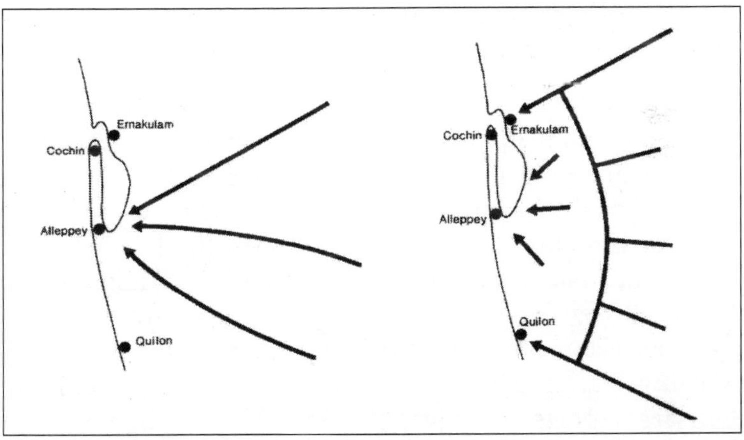

Figure 3.4: Transportation routes around Alleppey, before 1860 and around 1900. Sketchmap drawn by Hans Schenk/Jan ter Haar (University of Amsterdam).

were laid far beyond Alleppey but were directed towards other seaports. These new routes formed serious threats to the commodity flow to the town, a threat that became mainly manifest after 1900.

There were more threats. The increasing sizes of (notably steam) ships led to a growing reluctance among shippers to call at the port of Alleppey in case of a limited amount of cargo and of the port-dues to be paid (RAT 1888-9: 169). Obviously, economies of scale gave rise to this reported reluctance, and, even more, to an emerging disparity between technical improvements in shipping in the form of larger and more steam-driven ships, and the still limited amount of cargo that had to be shipped.[12] This signal to the future of the port of Alleppey had to be taken seriously, and it was done. From about 1900 onwards the position of the port was under discussion and it was seriously challenged. The threats resulted in two—opposing—trends:

(a) the desire, or the need to concentrate on the shipping facilities along the coast of Malabar, and thus to keep pace with the economies of scale of providing more sizeable quantities of cargo per port, and
(b) the desire to have a better equipped port in order to meet the demands of larger and more time-bound steamers.

The first threat, to concentrate port facilities, was of course relevant for all the ports along the coast of Malabar. Alleppey was a major port along this coast, along with Cochin, (or rather: British Cochin, a strategically located enclave in the State of Cochin) Calicut and Tellicherry (both in Malabar district of Madras Province), and a number of minor ones: Colachel (near Trivandrum) and Quilon in Travancore, and Badagra, Cannanore, Ponnani, Beypore and some others in Malabar district. Though the desire to concentrate on fewer but larger ports was there, it did not result in action. It led rather to competition by each port authority to win the race. The second threat, the desire to have 'better' ports seemed more tangible. It was operationalized in terms of the provision of quays along deep water[13] instead of roadsteads, the installation of power-driven cranes, etc. Such harbours required water inlets along the coast. In Alleppey an attempt was made to create an artificial water inlet by trying to extend Commercial Canal right into the Arabian Sea, but this failed. Natural water inlets had to be considered as more feasible possibilities to comply with such demands. Among the naturally existing inlets, the choice fell upon Cochin, partly for military reasons as was seen in Chapter 1. Partly too because of the central location of Cochin at the centre of the Malabar coast, the existing railway connection at its neighbouring place Ernakulam, its accessibility from a large hinterland by roads such as the MC Road in Travancore, and still by its nearby waterways (the backwaters). Its main drawback was a sand-bank just off the coast that prevented any sizeable ship to enter the basin that had to be transformed into a port.[14]

The choice was made to develop Cochin, but there is some confusion when the decision to transform 'Cochin' into a 'modern' port was made. What matters here is that the Government of Travancore decided in the 1890s not to continue to develop the Alleppey port any longer, as I mentioned above, but to give preference to the existing facilities at Cochin and its future prospects (see Government of Kerala, 1975: 586).

Robert Bristow, the main 'architect' of the port of Cochin, comments on this decision of Travancore that:

> . . . the merchants and others at Alleppey and Quilon strongly resisted the export and import of any Travancore cargo via Cochin and instead became more active competitors, so that there arose the anomalous position of a rival mercantile community opposing Cochin while the state itself (Travancore, HS) was making contribution to its further development and receiving one third of the Customs Revenue from the port. (Bristow, 1959: 183)

The plea, from the side of the British Resident in Travancore to develop Quilon, which has a similar natural water inlet, was never pursued, and the same administrative report in which the suggestion about Quilon was recorded, mentions that Cochin remained the favourite port for Travancore along the south-western coast (RAT, 1899-1900). It took twenty-five years before full political agreement was reached to start the works at Cochin (see Chapter 3). Meanwhile, the port of Alleppey was doomed to decay from the 1890s onwards, though on a rather long-term notice, as shall be seen in Chapter 4.

ALLEPPEY AT THE CROSSROADS OF TWO ERAS: ITS SOCIO-ECONOMIC PROFILE IN 1901

It was seen above that from the late 1800s onwards, signals could be observed about the worn-out lifelines of Alleppey. But signals of a new future could be seen as well: the emergence of industrial production and subsequent shipment of coir products. The census of 1901 (Census of India 1901, 1903) provides for an outstanding and rare opportunity to get an insight into the population of Alleppey, and notably, in the working population engaged in trade and transport of the long-standing export products and in the emerging coir industry. Here, some main conclusion will be given in a summarized form:

Compared to the other census towns in Travancore in 1901, Alleppey had a distinct profile as a trading and transporting town: 17 per cent of the workers and their dependents found a living in 'Commerce, Transport and Storage' against twelve percent for the average of the nine census town in Travancore.[15] 'Civil servants' (3 per cent against 11 per cent on average) and 'Professions' (7 per cent against 10 per cent on average) were markedly absent. Other occupational categories were neither extremely well nor extremely poorly represented in the as yet small town of about 25,000 inhabitants. Looking at a more detailed classification of types of jobs, a limited number of types of work can be found which were (a) relatively concentrated in Alleppey from a comparative Travancorean point of view, and which were (b) quantitatively dominant in the local composition of the labour force. Jobs related to water transport and port activities were, as could be expected outstandingly represented in a comparative perspective. Forty-six per cent of all 'Water-transport' jobs in the census towns in Travancore, were to be found in Alleppey. However, these types of jobs did not involve large shares of the working population. On the other hand, coir manufacturing did not clearly come to the fore in 1901 as an important means of subsistence for the local population (763 persons and their dependents were working in this field, 34 per cent of the Travancore total). Precise conclusions about the prevalence of industrial coir workers in Alleppey are obscured by an additional census-category of a non-differentiated mass of 'General labourers' as the main share of 'non-agricultural unskilled workers' and their dependents in the census (over 5,000 involved persons, 22 per cent of the total for the nine census towns), and some of these 'General labourers' may have been workers in the coir industry. But anyhow it seems that the economic profile of Alleppey in 1901 was more oriented toward trade and transport than toward industry.

The lack of artisans and professionals among the working population should be mentioned as well. This adds to the 'artificial' position of Alleppey, not embedded in a regional economic structure but mainly geared to domestic extraction, collection and transport to overseas destinations of a limited number of commodities: basically, spices and some products of the plantation industries.

Alleppey appeared to be a link in a chain in an extraction-oriented export economy, but not much more than a link. Its industrial base had yet to grow, and in some respects the local economy may have resembled that of colonial port towns such as Bombay or Calcutta before the 1860s.

NOTES

1. Quoted from the Alleppey District Gazetteer: Government of Kerala, 1975, Trivandrum, pp. 295-6. See also Aiya, 1906-III: 220-3.
2. In the 1970s a saltwater barrier was built between the largest inland lake (Vembanad Lake) and the northern sea inlet, about 20 km north-east of Alleppey, at Thannermukkom. This barrier has turned the lake and the adjoining Kuttanad area from a brackish into a freshwater basin. Moreover, at Thottapally, south of Alleppey, a storm water barrier has been built. These two infrastructural works

have changed the ecology of the backwater system considerably. See for further details: Government of Kerala, 1974.

3. In a letter which I received from a retired employee of the Swiss Trading firm Volkart Brothers (30 May 1980) the meaning of the mud bank is given in the following words: 'At Alleppey there had been certain fortuitous circumstances which gave this Port a spell of prosperity. For quite a number of years the oily mudbanks of Alleppey afforded smooth-water anchorage for ships during the south-west monsoon, waves passing over the banks being diminished in height and lessened in velocity. It enables ships to work in shelter with a certain amount of safely during monsoon.' There exists a wide range of theories about the origin and the nature of this mudbank. Bristow, 1959, and Government of Kerala, 1975 deal with some of these theories.
4. The name Alappuzha is said to originate from blacksmiths formerly living along the water course: hence 'Blacksmith Canal'. The site of this old cluster is more or less at 'Old Bazar', near Stone Bridge (see Figure 6.1).
5. Several authors give an account of this era, sometimes in the same wordings, e.g. Aiya (1906); Pillai (1935); Pillai (1940); Das Gupta (1967); Government of Kerala (1975); and Bernard (1977).
6. See Appendix, Table 1 for trade and transport statistics between 1865 and 1900.
7. The pepper trade, though, has been highly erratic and vulnerable to market fluctuations ever since it began.
8. The start of Darragh's endeavour is memorized in the following, anonymous text: 'He was the first European to start this work in Alleppey and it is due to him that the spinners were taught to spin yarn by machine instead of only by hand, from where he went on to the manufacture of Coir Mats & Matting. According to tradition, his Factory Superintendent—a Mr. Collins—was so closely imitated by his weavers that all Mats & Matting are woven with the left hand as Collins himself was lefthanded'.
9. This figure is exaggerated according to Jeffrey who quotes a much lower figure from the Travancore Almanac from 1891: 37,500 acres (15,800 ha), divided among 100 European planters and about 100 estates (Jeffrey, 1976: 105).

10. A detailed examination of primary sources is far beyond the scope of the study.
11. Jibin Mathew even states that the policy of the government of Travancore was not to extend the railway system, 'because of the cheaper backwater communication, which from one end of the state to the other . . . could . . . replace all other forms of transport especially in respect of heavy loads. (based on a file of 1942 from the Public Works Department of the state (2019: 110).
12. However, the trade statistics do not confirm this observed disparity as is shown in Appendix, Table 1. As a major part of the traditional cargo to be shipped overseas consisted of precious goods, like pepper and as the bulk cargoes (coir goods) were as yet of limited importance, or were shipped by coastal vessels to other ports at the subcontinent (copra, coconut oil), there was apparently not enough cargo to attract shippers to call at Alleppey. However, the decline was soon outmatched by increased coir goods and other bulk exports (see Chapter 4). Thus, around 1890, two opposing tendencies can be seen; the decline of the port as a spice-outlet—also due to the exhausted means to match 'economies of scale' with technical port facilities—and the advent of cheap bulk cargo, for which the port could function in a satisfactory way.
13. At that time a depth of 35 ft (10.67 meters) was required.
14. Bristow gives a detailed account of the off-shore dredging works to cut a 'canal' through the mud bank, of not less than 'three miles long, 450 ft wide, giving 35 ft at low water' (1959: 171) exclaiming when the works were accomplished in 1928: 'Cochin was open to sea-going vessels!' (ibid.: 170).
15. These figures present approximations rather than certainties. The meaning of 'dependent' is, e.g. obscure, while no insight is given in part-time work in different types of jobs.

CHAPTER 4

Growth and Decline of a Low-cost Economy: Alleppey Since 1900

THE COIR INDUSTRY

In the preceding chapter a conclusion has been drawn that a number of opposing trends characterized Alleppey's economic position at the brink of the twentieth century. The importance of Alleppey's port remained unchallenged in Travancore as it was anchored in the still far dominant inland water transport of relevant cargo for the overseas trade, even as it became outdated. However: new roads and railroads emerged: far away from the town. Manufacturing (of coir products) was still in its infancy around 1900, but there was scope for expansion, given the abundance of raw materials from the coconut tree in the immediate region, and given the growing demand for coir products. These products had to be transported, inland and via the port, thus promoting a continuation of outdated trends. These contradictions make it necessary to have at first a closer look at Alleppey's coir industry.

The technical and organizational structure of the coir industry in the twentieth century has been described and analysed in detail in several publications.

The 1961 Census of India publications include a very detailed monograph on the processing and the marketing structure of coir (Census of India 1961, 1964: 75-132). A survey undertaken by the Coir Board in 1960 provides a detailed account of the various stages in the production process, and of the positions of the workers involved in these stages of production (Coir Board, 1963). Unnithan (1970 and 1972) reported in detail on the economic aspects of the coir industry. As early as 1955, the then Government of Travancore-Cochin published a report on the industry (Government of Travancore-Cochin, 1955). In addition, a range of authors have dealt with aspects of the coir industry (see, e.g. Gulati, 1981: 136-64; Jeffrey, 1984; Isaac, 1982, 1985). Its main characteristics are outlined in the 1961Census-monograph:

> The coir industry in Kerala consists of two types, the cottage type and the factory type, which also synchronize with two stages of the industry. Up to and including the production of coir yarn the industry partakes the nature of either the cottage type or the small scale industrial establishments employing but a small number of workers. This sector of the industry may be called the spinning sector and takes in such operations as collection, retting and beating of coconut husks, cleaning the fibre and production of coir yarn. From this stage the industry branches itself into three main groups, namely, those engaged in the purchase, curing and pressing of yarn into bales for export, those producing mat, matting carpets, rugs and similar products for both export and internal consumption, and those producing ropes or cables of small, medium and large sizes for local consumption or for export. (Census of India 1961, 1964: 77)

In addition to this listing, it is useful to remember that the factory type of coir production is rather recent, having started after 1860, while the cottage type and the export of yarn and rope is said to go back at least to the thirteenth century.

Factory-wise coir production, in particular the processing of mats, etc., is associated with a few phenomena which have been relevant to Alleppey, especially when it reached its highest peak during the 1920s and 1930s. It was

(a) urban-based (in Alleppey, in the nearby smaller town of Shertallai, and to some extent in places like Cochin and Calicut),
(b) it was undertaken in large-scale processing units, contrary to the cottage-type productions;

(c) it included machinery (looms, etc.);
(d) it had been initiated and dominated (till the mid-1950s) by foreign entrepreneurs;
(e) it brought industrial capitalist modes of production into the town;
(f) new products were fabricated from the coir yarn;
(g) it concentrated on end-products for export (mats, etc., mainly) and less on exporting semi-finished products (yarn) for final processing abroad; and
(h) it was very much export oriented.

Some of these phenomena are relevant for the subject of this chapter and will be discussed here. Others refer to the changing social structure of the town [points (d) and (e)] and are embedded in Chapter 5.

Why has the factory production of coir products become urban? There is no clear answer in terms of the physical- and economic-geographical conditions in and around Alleppey. Since the first stage of the processing of coir (from husk to yarn) is rural and widely dispersed over large tracts in lowland Travancore, Cochin and Malabar district, factories could just as conveniently be located somewhere close to any first-stage site of production. Final products of this first-stage production could subsequently be sent to any of the several ports along the coast. Given the 'neutrality' of sites in these terms, it is most likely that urban sites were considered more convenient to (foreign) entrepreneurs. Alleppey and other urban places had not much to offer in terms of facilities during the late 1800s and the early 1900s, but nevertheless they were in company of a few fellow-foreigners (at least the Commercial Agent of the state in Alleppey!). And, as far as Alleppey is concerned, the decision of James Darragh to settle there and start a factory, may have been by chance, but may have influenced others, eventually leading to some concentration of this new form of coir-processing in the town. In addition, it is possible that labour was more easily available in the town than in the countryside.

Factory processing was undertaken on a large scale as long as the (foreign) entrepreneurs were able to so. They had access to capital (both in India and in Great Britain) and they had access to consumers' markets. The cottage industrials were not in such a position. The small-scale producers described themselves as *muthalali*s (capitalist employers), but overall, they must be considered as a 'glorified type of workers' (Census of India 1961, 1964: 101), without much scope to enlarge their businesses. And even within the class of factory entrepreneurs, the Indians among them before Second World War were not in a position to compete with the Europeans in terms of the scale of the enterprises. Aspiring foreign entrepreneurs could create markets and subsequently purvey to the increased demand, and they were willing to do so. Their risks were not great: labour worked on contract basis: mats, etc., were manufactured per order and not in advance. Capital investments were there, but these were limited as well. Besides, Schumacher's words that small is beautiful were yet unspoken.

The actual scale of operations in the urban coir-factorize was uncertain and fluctuating. The fluctuations stemmed from the fact that besides the clerical staff and a few regular labourers, there were not many workers on the permanent payroll till the end of the Second World War. Independent middlemen brought workers into the factory premises based on job contracts between the factory and the middlemen, as was quite customary in Indian industries. On the compounds of each of the eight large-scale factories in Alleppey and its immediate surroundings in the 1930s, were found at least 500 workers in (ir)regular employment, while this figure rose sometimes to 2,000 workers in some factories. Medium-sized factories (mostly Indian owned) employed directly and indirectly much smaller numbers of workers. These units mainly prepared semi-finished goods on contract basis with the large-scale units. The latter provided the final treatment, such as shearing of the mats, and shipped them. In this way the large companies were as much manufacturing companies as trading firms.

The dichotomy formed by a few large-scale and a few more middle-scale urban units, in contrast to the very many small-scale rural production units, is reflected in the degree of mechanization of the production process of the coir goods. The rural sites of production and the rural stages of production were dominated by manual labour,[1] while the urban stages of production were more machine-based. The difference should, however, not be overestimated. Winnowing and a part of the spinning of the fibre has been done in the countryside for many decades by hand-operated machinery. The manufacture of mats, etc., depends on looms, mainly hand looms, and according to observers in 1961, it is of a primitive character (Census of India 1961, 1964: 101). Power looms were virtually absent before the Second World War, while a few steam and oil-powered engines were mainly used for dyeing and for bailing yarn. In both stages of the processing, labour outweighed capital investment as a factor of production. On the other hand, without even this primitive degree of mat weaving the industry would not have started and developed in Alleppey after Darragh's initiative in 1859.

Mechanization of coir production has been a vital issue in and around Alleppey for a long time and its extent and intensity has aroused many disputes. The mechanization of fibre processing from retted husk was tried even in the early 1900s, but it failed on economic grounds: labour proved to be too cheap! (Isaac, 1983; Schampers, 1984, p. 50). Besides, labour was fostered. The 1911 Census Commissioner considered manual labour as a prerequisite for a vital and strong population. Machines should be avoided, as jealousy arising from concentration of wealth associated with capital investments would be the result (Census of India 1911, Part I, 1912: 69-70). This outburst conformed strikingly to Gandhian views of economy and society. After the Second World War the installation of power looms was opposed bitterly and in the main successfully resisted by organized labour (Isaac, 1983; see for this struggle for employment also Chapter 5). It can be stated that both before and after the Second World War, the factory-based coir industry was rooted in rather primitive technical conditions, while (cheap) labour was widely available and made use of.

TRANSPORT OF COIR TO AND FROM ALLEPPEY

Technical conditions also played a role in the transport of coir products in the several stages of transformation from husk to mats and ropes. It was shown in Chapter 3 that the hinterland of Alleppey had shrunk because of the development of overland transport facilities. The transport of pepper and other products from the hills and the midlands tended to be diverted to more easily accessible ports. The 'coconut-economy' was very much confined to the lowlands and for a great deal concentrated in and around the backwater region, immediately beyond Alleppey and a few other places.

Water transport remained not only the most 'natural' way of transporting coir products during the several stages of production, but it remained also almost the only way, as there

Figure 4.1: Vellam unloading coir yarn at Commercial Canal for industrial processing. (Photograph by Volkart Brothers).

was no good alternative due to the absence of roads. Even in 1960, and throughout Kerala, 60 per cent of all transports of coir goods was carried out by inland boats, 5 per cent by headloaders, 25 per cent by bullock carts and only 10 per cent by other means—including trucks (Unnithan, 1970: 135-6, derived from 1960 Economic and Statistical Survey of the Coir Board). As these figure pertain to the whole of Kerala and are rather recent, it may be safely assumed that before the Second World War the region of Alleppey relied almost completely on: 'incredibly slow and incredibly cheap', inland water transport (Ouwerkerk, 1994: 165).

As the bulk of the finished and semi-finished coir products was exported to places far beyond the subcontinent, seaports obviously played a key role as media for forward linkages. The port of Alleppey became such a medium. It is largely through coir exports that the turnover of the port grew amazingly during the first three decades of the 1900s, and again for some time after the Second World War (see Appendix, Tables 2 and 3). This growth was there despite signs of decay and in spite of increasing competition from Cochin.

In absolute numbers the annual tonnage of ships plying the port rose to about 250,000 to 350,000 ton during the late 1890s, as Table 1 of the Appendix shows. Available statistics show a gap till the end of First World War, but it can be assumed shipping was rather poor during the first two decades of the 1900s. Several remarks in the annual reports on the Administration of Travancore point in that direction as well (see, e.g. the RAT for the years 1903-4; 1909-10; and 1917-18). After the First World War shipping increased rapidly. Especially many more steamships called at the port: some hundred around 1920 against 350 to 450 between the late 1920s and late 1930s.[2] As can subsequently be expected: the annual shipping capacity rose also. It was less than about 200,000 tons around 1920 and increased to more than a million tons in 1930. This level was more or less maintained during the 1930s but fell to nil during the Second World War. In the absence of available statistics, no detailed account can be given of the composition of the exports. At the beginning of the twentieth century all coconut-tree products contributed to about 50 per cent of the value of the export trade via Alleppey. Coir products alone in the late 1930s contributed 40 per cent of the value of all exports, and after the Second World War this share increased to 75 or even 80 per cent. Since coir products had a relatively low intrinsic value in terms of the rupee value per ton, or a similar measure, and much lower than spices, it can be safely assumed that the port of Alleppey was mainly serving as an outlet for coir products from the early 1900s onward. From a spice outlet since the 1760s and the greater part of the 1800s, the port had become a coir-port.[3]

The factory-based coir industry—as it flourished between the world wars—can be characterized as an industry on low costs of production under rather primitive conditions, while it made use of cheap but rather primitive inland water-transportation. To this can be added that Alleppey was a cheap port as well, in terms of port duties. This conjunction of low costs of production and of transportation created favourable conditions for the expansion of the coir industry and its related transport, and for economic growth in Alleppey as a whole.

COPRA AND COCONUT OIL

The coir industry can be characterized as having a low technical base, which partly explains its growth. The coconut oil industry, probably Alleppey's second largest industrial sector (though much smaller than the coir industry) shows the same pattern. This industry stems from the same coconut tree as the coir industry, but it treats the kernel itself out of which the dried pulp—copra—is crushed to collect oil. This oil has a wide variety of applications, from hair oil to frying oil. The processing of oil has a long tradition, but since the late 1800s it has gained momentum by the mechanization of the extraction process whereby animate power and steam power are used. The efficiency of the extraction process is low, and the industry lost much of its importance after the development of more efficient techniques of oil extraction. These more capital-intensive techniques were applied in Bombay. The Alleppey mill owners found these techniques too costly and subsequently shifted much of their business towards shipping copra to Bombay instead of extracting and shipping oil.[4] The development of this industry is not further dealt with here.

ALLEPPEY'S LOW-COST ECONOMY: AN INTERIM ASSESSMENT

There is a basic factor in Alleppey's economic development after 1900, and its relation to technical progress. Its traditional trade and transport drifted gradually away to Cochin from the late 1800s onwards, though this process was compensated by an overall expansion of trade, both from Alleppey and from other ports along the coast of Malabar. As a result, relative decline but absolute growth continued after 1900, when for example the pepper trade could bring substantial profits to entrepreneurs and the state exchequer for a couple of years. Pepper exports were overshadowed, however, even in the late 1800s by coir exports. Among the latter, more end products were found: mats, matting, carpets, rugs and rope, in addition to yarn, copra and coconut oil. The expansion of all these branches had one thing in common it was based on cheap and primitive means of production and distribution, i.e. cheap labour and low capital investments. Moreover, the coir industry provided a relatively cheap floor covering for homes in the Western world, which made the product rather crisis-resistant (the coir industry and its exports suffered relatively little during the worldwide economic crisis of the 1930s; see also Jeffrey, 1984). The coir industry provided a relatively inferior product, almost to the point of being substandard. The entrepreneurs were aware of this situation. Langley noted a deterioration in quality of coir mats, etc. (probably before the Second World War) and he blamed the 'crude' mechanization of the spinning process in Malabar district (Langley, n.d.: 47-9). These aspects of the coir industry explain, however in part, its vulnerability. Moreover, since the 1930s labourers started to demand higher wages and they thus also threatened the low-cost circuit which meant poverty for many, in which the industry and its entrepreneurs prospered, as shall be seen in some later chapters.

Low costs of transportation also implied slow means of transportation, and this mattered more and more when time became an equivalent for money in business circles. The direct road connection to Cochin, which was completed in the 1950s, therefore brought some of the finished products to Cochin's port, by trucks to the quays and cranes of the modern port, and as an alternative to the complex and also slow process of lighterage to ships on the roadstead of Alleppey. And, when after the Second World War, the European, American and Australian consumers could afford more expensive and luxurious floor coverings, coir products were largely bypassed and forgotten, and thus the exports decreased. When attempts were made to implement more sophisticated machinery (e.g. power looms) in preparing mats, etc., labourers fought for employment and against machines. Similarly, trucks and quays and cranes threatened the *vellam* and lighters at the Alleppey roadstead, just as sophisticated coconut-oil extraction processes in Bombay threatened primitive though cheap processes in Alleppey.

The economy of Alleppey was entrenched in cheapness, and it prospered in circuits of low-cost production, distribution, and even consumption of its export products. This was the strength and also the weakness of the local economy of Alleppey. It was its strength as long as its conditions (societal, technical) were not challenged, but its weakness if they were. Alleppey was a giant on clay feet, so to speak, exploited by a few.

THE COLLAPSE OF THE ECONOMY OF ALLEPPEY: WEAKNESSES OF ITS LOW-COST

After the Second World War, the inevitable came: the economy collapsed, and did so rather rapidly, though during a few years in the 1950s it showed some signs of recovery from the war-time stagnation. The available statistics show the collapse in several ways and point at varying causes, working in isolation and in combination, as shall be seen in the following sections.

The Port of Cochin

The growing importance of 'Cochin' is the first cause of 'Alleppey's' economic collapse. This became clear after the war: Cochin developed into a sizeable port serving the import and export trade for large areas in south India, and it became one of the 'major ports' of the newly-independent country. The port of Cochin became equipped with modern port facilities and with a better infrastructure. During the 1930s the significance of the port was of the same magnitude as that of Alleppey and Calicut in terms of numbers of steamers and their tonnage calling at the ports. For the post-war years there are no direct similar comparative statistical data available, but a comparison in terms of the rupee value of the export and import trade during the period 1951-2 to 1969-70 shows that of all the ports of Kerala, Cochin handled about 80 to 90 per cent of the foreign trade to and from the combined hinterlands, while for the two next biggest ports—Alleppey and Calicut—only a few percents remained (Government of Kerala, 1972).[5] Regarding imports the role of Alleppey seems to have ended in the mid-1960s.

The overall decline of trade and transport at the port of Alleppey can be seen in more detail in Table 3 of the Appendix. This table shows the number of steamers and other ships and their tonnage given for the post-war years till 1974. It will be seen that after a short revival, the port was virtually closed around 1970. At the end of the 1970s, basic facilities as lighters and tugs were not available anymore. An occasional ship intending to call at the port made it necessary for the Port Authority to ask for assistance from Quilon or Cochin.

The Decline of Overseas Demand for Coir Products

A second cause for the collapse of the local economy is to be found in the declining overseas markets for coir goods. This simple fact is obscured however, by a number of (temporarily) conflicting tendencies of several kinds.[6] Table 4 of the Appendix tabulates the export of coir goods for the three coir-exporting ports in present-day Kerala (and in India!), Alleppey, Calicut and Cochin, again for the 1950s and 1960s (no comparative data are available for the 1970s). In Table 4 a further distinction is made for type of coir products: unfinished goods (mainly yarn and some fibre) and finished goods (mats, matting, etc., and some rope). An analysis of the data in Tables 1-3 for all ports together shows an increase in the export of both unfinished goods and finished goods till about 1964 and a subsequent decline. The decline of the unfinished goods is heavy, that of the finished goods slight. For Cochin and Alleppey separately (Calicut plays hardly a role), one can see for Cochin again a rise in the export of unfinished goods till the late 1950 and a subsequent decline. There is a low but steady increase of finished goods exported from Cochin. The picture for Alleppey shows signs of an opposite trend: first a rise in the export of unfinished goods, followed by a slight decline only, while the export of finished goods continued to decline.

Alleppey's ability to increase its exports of yarn can be related to two developments in the Western world. After the Second World War in Europe the mechanized manufacturing of mats and matting expanded. This created a demand for yarn and suppressed the demand for the Alleppey-made mats, matting, rugs and carpets. Since the 1960s, the Western demand for coir goods decreased. The export of yarn decreased accordingly. Also, another conclusion regarding the export of finished and unfinished coir goods can be drawn. This conclusion refers to the export-route taken in Kerala. The port of Cochin was able to attract almost all exports of finished articles, while the port of Alleppey managed to handle more and more of the yarn. This 'specialization' symbolizes the role of Alleppey in international trade and manufacturing. In a preceding section in this chapter Alleppey's role been has described and explained, as being embedded in a circuit of low-cost: low costs of labour, low costs of transport, low capital investments, and on catering for a relatively 'low budget' consumption abroad. Every attempt at sophistication of an aspect in this circuit, was bound to affect Alleppey's role in a negative way. Technical modernization in the form of infrastructural developments favoured Cochin; increased purchasing power in the Western world affected the coir industry in general. The same applies for the increasing costs of labour (see Chapter 5). Thus, when Cochin developed into a modern port it took away the most precious items on the list of coir goods, while the cheap and inconvenient port of Alleppey could survive for the time being by relying on the export of semi-raw materials. The diminished overseas-demand for yarn caused this last bastion of the port to fade away. State statistics of the early 1970s show a decline to next to nothing.[7] The meagre kingdom collapsed at last.

The decline of the export of coir goods has led to a decline in its production as well as the home market for such goods was insignificant. Industrial production, especially that of finished products, but also that of coconut oil declined sharply. In Table 4.1 the decline of the medium- and large-sized coir

TABLE 4.1 MIDDLE- AND LARGE-SIZED COIR FACTORIES IN ALLEPPEY, ACCORDING TO THE NUMBER OF WORKERS, 1964 TO 1977

Number of Workers	*1964*	*1977*
20-49	4	13
50-99	13	6
100-249	4	4
250-499	7	–
500 +	4	–
Total number of units	32	23
Total number of workers	5,030	1,268

Sources: Data taken with permission of Bureau of Economic and Statistics, Alleppey branch.

factories, which catered for the bulk of the finished products, is shown for the period between 1964 and 1977.

Similar other data confirm this picture of a disappearing industry, obviously together with a disappearing source of labour. Prakash (1977: 30) quotes from a report by the Coir Advisory Board of 1970: 'While in the early 40s the number of workers in the mats and matting manufacturing industry was 35,000, at present there are only 2,500 workers in the organized sector.' The loss of employment in the organized coir-industry[8] was partly compensated by an increasing number of small-scale and household-scale units. Some large-scale companies found it preferable to buy 'home-made' coir goods and ship them after giving a finishing touch. This practice existed also in earlier period in the history of coir production, but it grew in importance. The large-scale units could thus work with a very small staff. The combination of local, regional and global trends resulted in Alleppey in large-scale underemployment and idleness in the numerous small-scale industries, and massive unemployment in all types of the coir industry.

De-industrialization of Alleppey

Any conclusion regarding Alleppey's economy since the 1950s must unavoidably be couched in sad wordings. It relates to the collapse of the pillars on which its economy rested, the export of spices and the coir industry. This conclusion should also convey another observation. The shift in coir exports from finished to semi-finished products under conditions of a general decline of the export of coir products, marks a process of modern de-industrialization in Alleppey.

The term de-industrialization refers to an ongoing debate, on an all-India level, about whether the former colony underwent a process of decline of artisan-based industrial activities as a result of British colonization (see for an overview Charlesworth, 1982). The debate focuses on the 1800s, while there is a broad consensus that after the First World War a (counter) movement of modest industrialization started, largely carried out by Indian entrepreneurs (Gadgil, 1971; Kulkarni, 1971). As far as the nineteenth century is concerned, there is also a consensus that the industrial pattern in India changed from catering to a world market of finished luxury products to the supply of raw material and semi-finished good to Western industries.

Modern de-industrialization in Alleppey refers to a different pattern. While de-industrialization in India in the 1800s concentrated on the decline of indigenous handicraft industries, in Alleppey a dismantling of mainly foreign large-scale manufacturing units took place after the Second World War. It is tempting to relate this de-industrialization of Alleppey, to the departure of foreign entrepreneurs since the 1950s. For the time-being a co-incidence fits better. Anyway, in terms of large-scale historical patterns of industrial growth and decline in India, Alleppey came to fit the role of a dependent economy, delivering the raw materials for industrial finalizing elsewhere. However, Alleppey's path towards this role and the period in which this path was taken were quite unusual and can only be explained by stressing the local physical-geographical and political context, and the local conditions pertaining to manufacturing and transport.

It adds to the significance of local factors in explaining processes of (de-) industrialization that during the decades in which the final blows were given to the industrial economy of Alleppey, only 80 km south of this town—in and around Quilon—a new and indigenous industrial export sprang up. This sector dealt with the roasting and packing of cashew nuts, partly grown locally, partly imported as 'raw cashew nuts' from East Africa (see James, 1981). Thus, within a short distance and under comparative socio-economic conditions, two developments took highly divergent courses, at variance with each other, and with alleged pre-destined roles of industrial export development in a Third World country in the post colonial era.

THE ISOLATION OF ALLEPPEY: OLD BACKWATERS AND NEW (RAIL) ROADS

Alleppey's recent economic history is not only the history of its (coir) export business, though this is a factor of vital importance, and its collapse was fatal. But in addition, other factors, especially in the sphere of transportation developments, continued to abet Alleppey's downfall. Land routes to 'feed' Alleppey and to make the town 'serve' its hinterland were hardly there. Attempts to bridge the Backwaters by constructing east-west running roads to Alleppey were made, but failed on the whole till the early 1980s, as the construction of a few major bridges proved to be a technical bottleneck. Alleppey remained still largely dependent on slow water transport to and from its immediate hinterland: a journey across the backwaters—say 20 km as the crow flies—would easily take two to three hours by car plus ferries, or by boat. Alleppey remained thus for all practical purposes cut off from commercial centres east of the backwaters, as well as from the produce of that region. On the other hand, routes 'feeding' Cochin have increased in number and quality. A railway line from Cochin to the south but east of the backwaters, crowned till the late 1980s the diversion of transportation routes from the midlands of Kerala to its new export outlet. It was only in 1989 that Alleppey got its long hoped-for railway connection with Cochin, and a few years later with the south of Kerala (see also Chapter 8).

Overland transportation routes have played an important role in discussions in Alleppey's business circles, at least since the 1950s. Road and railroad construction has often been used as a condition, perhaps a sufficient condition, to regain the business prosperity of former times: the absence of (rail) roads as a cause and sometime even a sufficient cause for the economic downfall of the town. Transport facilities rated high in the local analyses of Alleppey's past, present and future state, as will be seen in Chapter 7, where some societal perspectives on, and reactions to the changes which had taken place, will come to the fore.

NOTES

1. The manual part is quite specialized. The production of coir yarn takes place in units of three to ten workers. A small unit of four to five is the most common one. The process starts by buying the husks of 500 coconuts that have been left for about six months to ret in the brackish water of the ditches which abound in the village. The retting loosens the fibre from the wooden tissue of the coconut husks, The husks are first torn into 3 or 4 parts (*pola*), stamped with a long stick (*olakka*) and again kept in water till they are beaten into fiber. The softening of *pola*s with a stamper is work that takes about one day and is almost exclusively done by boys between twelve and sixteen, who are engaged on a piece rate of Rs. 4 for 500 husks. When taken from the water, each *pola* is again beaten to soften it, with a short, heavy wooden stick (*kootuvadi*) and the peeled. Afterwards it is beaten again and at again—with thirty to eighty blows—to separate the fibre from the grain. This part of the work takes about eighteen working days. The next step consists of winnowing either manually by shaking the fibre with two small bamboo sticks, or mechanically at the local mill. The spinning of yarn that is used to weave coco mats and matting—an industry located at Alleppey—is done with the help of a spinning wheel operated by two spinners and a worker that turns the main wheel. Spinning the fibre obtained from 500 husks takes about six to eight days and is a qualified work. The last operation, rolling and bundling the yarn, takes half a day (Schenk, 1984: 123).
2. The total tonnage plying at the port of Cochin was not substantially higher around 1930: about 1.2 to 1.3 million tons a year, while some 1,100 steamers called at that port (Census of India 1931, 1933: 153).
3. That means, naturally: regarding its exports. A wide range of industrial and other goods were imported, and notably Burmese rice.
4. See for more particulars: Government of Kerala, 1975: 226-8.
5. The combined hinterlands of these ports were of course not necessarily the same as those in earlier years. Cochin has probably

been more and more able to attract trade from a larger part of south India, far beyond the boundaries of Kerala State.

6. A full analysis of this factor cannot be made here. It also includes research in coir manufacturing and consumption patterns in the Western world where the largest numbers of consumers could be found.
7. The tonnage of finished products declined from about 5,000 tons in the 1960s to 1,000 in the mid-1970s; that of unfinished products from 15,000 tons in the mid-1960s to 6,000 tons a decade later.
8. This loss was to some extent related to the departure of the large-scale and often foreign-owned production units. See further in subsequent chapters.

PART TWO

SOCIETY, SPACE AND ENVIRONMENT

CHAPTER 5

Changes in the Social Structure of Alleppey

SOCIAL CHANGE IN TRAVANCORE AND ALLEPPEY IN THE 1700s

When in 1762 Raja Verma and his minister Kesava Das had started to build Alleppey on the site of a village called Alappuzha, they asked north Indian merchants to settle and trade in this new town: Parsis, Gujaratis, Kutchis and Sindhis. In addition, Chettiars came from present-day Tamil Nadu, Jews from Cochin and Parur, Konkani-Brahmins (refugees from Portuguese-held Goa) from several places along the Malabar coast, such as the former trading centre Purakkad (Porca). They were invited to come on very favourable terms: land along the dug Commercial Canal was given free, and rents for the use of state warehouses were low. Temples and mosques were built by the state.

Why were such generous terms offered to 'foreign' (though 'Indian') merchants? Kesava Das obviously wanted a strong merchant community in order to beat the European trading companies in the long run. By inviting merchant from various parts, he could forge trading bonds with many parts of the subcontinent. But the invitation implied also that in Travancore no merchants were available who could deal successfully with overseas trade. Even the internal trade of Travancore was at that time very limited (Jeffrey 1976: 32) and—significantly enough—mainly undertaken by non-Hindus, or at least non-Malayali Hindus: Syrian Christians (descendants of high-caste converts to Christianity in the first century AD), Muslims, Tamil Chettiars, some Tamil Brahmins, besides the Konkani-Brahmin immigrants. This marks the fact that traditional Keralese Hinduism lacked a clear *varma* of traders. As it is put in the 1921 census:

> . . . and the absence of a place for the trader class must be attributed to the want of necessity for such an occupation, on the general principle that function precedes organisation. (Census of India 1921-I; 1922: 19)

The Syrian Christians especially rose to prominence during the eighteenth century, and they secured major shares of the inland state trading monopolies which were installed at that time (see Bayly 1984: 188-9). Under these state trading regimes, state agents were sanctioned to buy produce meant for export, such as spices and timber from agriculturalists at fixed prices and have it transported to the Alleppey warehouses where it was auctioned by the state department of trade to the foreign bidders. During the 1700s trading under state control was promoted in the process of state formation of Travancore (see also Chapter 2) and it is hardly an exaggeration to state that a 'trading community' was created. This was of course even more true for Alleppey since the town was purposefully created as a focal point for trade.

The 'modernization' of Travancore's society as an element of the strategies of state building during the 1700s (Bayly, 1984) thus included a marked re-configuration of that society at the top: traders were more or less introduced to it and they were given a prominent place. At the bottom, less change took place during the eighteenth and the early decades of the nineteenth centuries. For the large majority of the population extreme caste barriers and extreme feudal dependencies governed their existence. Lowest ranking were the 'slave castes' as the Pulayas and the Parayas among whom untouchability and slavery were combined. For the higher prescribed societal positions, a complicated system was devised for the regulation of interactions among the several castes and religious groups. 'Pollution' took in this system an all-important place, and clothing and housing regulations and privileges formed the visual stigmata to denote one's place in society—from Brahmins via Nayar to Ezhava agricultural workers and to slaves. In this complex system participated non-Hindus as castes as well, as Fuller has shown (1976) and they also had to acquiesce to the rules of behaviour prescribed to castes. Jeffrey wrote, e.g.:

> Unlike Nayars, Syrian men wore their hair close cut, but they assumed the right of shoulder cloth and the umbrella. (1976: 18)[1]

It was the Syrian Christians who, as state traders, controlled the commercial department of the state in Alleppey, and found there their counterparts from elsewhere in India. The first stage of the process of social structuring of Alleppey is thus marked by the creation of an elite of both foreign traders and Syrian Christians. At the bottom of the local ladder were the workers, whose task it was to load the sea-going ships, to row or to pole the *vellam* and to garble pepper. Not much is known about them. It is said in Alleppey by old inhabitants that at that time people were afraid to board sea-going ships and that workers were taken by force: they were probably slaves. Moreover, life-term prisoners were taken from jails to work in these ships. Needless to say, that the social relations were extremely skewed and the sharing of power extremely one-sided. In this manner started Alleppey more as a convict camp than as a trading colony. But what changes took place during the 1800s?

SOCIAL CHANGE IN THE 1800s IN TRAVANCORE: MISSIONARIES AND CAPITALISTS

The question that arises in the first place is in which way and in which sequence did the *de facto* British rule over Travancore since around 1800 influence the social pattern of Alleppey. There is not much information to be found regarding the position and the power of Robert Gordon, the first British Commercial Agent in Alleppey, in charge of the commercial department of Travancore, or of his successors during the first half of the nineteenth century. One is inclined to conclude from this lack of information that the British top of the commercial department just superseded the Syrian Christian management of it, without much interference in the internal wing of the activities of the state trading department, run by the *sirkar* (government) agents. The concern of the Commercial Agent was—on behalf of the East India Company—to increase the pepper trade and to control its price. On the other hand, the fixed prices offered by the Travancore *sirkar*-agents for pepper and other spices encouraged the smuggling out of the country to free trade markets where higher prices were offered. Consequently, the pepper supply to Alleppey fell from the 1830s onwards (Jeffrey, 1976: 32; 63; Lemercinier 1983: 209). Under these conditions the Commercial Agent had to serve opposing policies, and subsequently he may have been in an ambivalent position. His position became clearer when free trade was imposed on Travancore from the 1860s onwards.

More fundamental for later changes in the social structure of Travancore and of Alleppey were the missionary activities undertaken since the 1810s by the London Missionary Society (LMS) and the Church Missionary Society (CMS) in Travancore. These societies were—more than any other organization at that time—involved in abolishing slavey in Travancore.

The major impact of slavery was on agricultural labour: in 1836 about 165,000 'soil slaves' (*adiyar*) and other slaves were counted (RRSC-I 1970: 57) in a population of 1.3 million.[2] The system of slavery was gradually abolished during the first half of the 1800s. The slave trade was already forbidden during the first decade of British suzerainty, but it took more than thirty years before—in 1847—the abolition of the system was asked for in a petition from missionaries. The answer came in 1854 in the form of long-term abolitions: all future descendants of slaves were declared to be free. One year later, however, slavery was officially abolished. Accounts of this process have been given by RRSC, 1970; Jeffrey, 1976: 37-50; Kooiman, 1983; and Bayly, 1984.[3]

However, the missionary societies were also instrumental in starting social mobility for the slave castes (Kooiman, 1983: 368). In urban areas like Alleppey the abolition of slavery was also a first step towards the formation of class-oriented organizations of labourers, like trade unions. But it took a longtime before this materialized, as will be discussed later in this chapter. Comparable to slavery was the system of statute labour: gratuitous rendering of services, delivering of goods and forced labour for the benefit of the state and of private organizations (known as *oozhiyam* of *viruthy*). Statute labour was gradually abolished between 1865 and 1894 (RRSC-I, 1970: 59-60). The abolition of slavery and statute labour marks the very gradual change in Travancore from a feudal society towards the beginning of a commercialized society with capitalist traits. Ascribed inequality gave in some respects way to inequality on the basis of achievement—according to the most idealistic views on the nature of this change.[4]

These developments fall in line with the struggle to remove the visible stigmata of inequality. The low-caste Shanar women, e.g., fought a prolonged battle to get permission to wear an upper cloth, which was allowed in 1859. In this case too, missionaries supported the Shanar women and opposed high-caste opposition to this impertinence (see Kooiman, 1983).

The emerging 'commercialized society' in Travancore, and its accompanying economy, in which capitalist modes of production made their entrance, is one manifestation of change.

> The establishment of large weaving mills was part of a process of capitalist transformation encouraged by the state of Travancore. Labour was freed from bondage and slavery, . . . foreign companies were given special concessions, obstacles for free trade were removed. . . . Travancore became a state with a highly liberal economic policy, attractive for foreign investors and contributing proportionally large sums to the British crown. (Schampers, 1984: 39-40)

The new cash economy, as Jeffrey puts it (1976: 32) was accompanied by the commercialization of agriculture which has been described by Namboodiripad (1967), Varghese (1970), Lemercinier (1983) and others, as mentioned in Chapter 2. This pertains to Alleppey in that since the 1860s, the increased foreign and domestic demand for coir was matched by increased coconut growing, more or less a monopoly of the low caste of the Ezhavas (or Iravas) who were the tenders, tappers and climbers of the coconut trees, and the soakers, ratters and spinners of the husk.[5] The Ezhavas could take advantage of the growing demand for their labour and that too in cash. Jeffry explains this advantage in the following lines:

> While cash was little used and the production of the coconut palm were not in great demand outside Kerala, these traditional occupations held little promise but drudgery. However, . . . when the demand for coconut products in Europe and America increased towards the end of the nineteenth-century, Iravas were able to take advantage of a cash economy, and their labour became indispensable to the merchants in towns like Alleppey. (1976: 21; see also 139-40)[6]

Expanding economic opportunities went together with increased possibilities for economic and social mobility. Since the end of the 1800s, particularly the Ezhavas, but also Pulayas and Shanars were able to seize the opportunity to attend formal secular education, which progressed rapidly since the 1870s but which was hardly accessible to the low castes till the close of the nineteenth century (see Tharakan, 1984). Converts and some Ezhavas went to Christian schools (and much earlier: a CMS girls' schools had been opened in Alleppey in 1825). But, after the 1880s and 1890s the Ezhavas went in increasing numbers to government schools. Around the same time, in 1903, the Ezhavas started a caste organization (the Sree Narayana Dharma Paripalana Yogam—SNDP) which also began to run its own educational institutions. The emancipation of the Ezhavas thus had a dual character. Partly it was based on 'modern' economic developments and more liberal views on society: the expansion of the cash economy influenced by the growth of the coir industry and the process of some change from ascription to achievement. Partly it turned out to be caste oriented as well and as such related to the well-known processes of Sanskritization in India (see Rajendran, 1974). 'Respectability' has been a keyword to understand the grievances of the low and slave castes. Some slave caste members found respectability in Christianity, other and especially the Ezhavas in raising consciousness. Both strategies brought low and slave caste members to grasp the opportunities offered through economic expansion in Travancore. These created the specific Travancorean and present-day Keralese mixture of class and caste adherences which have played and still play an important role in the social, economic and political history of the Alleppey region.

FROM CASH AND RESPECTABILITY TO CLASS AND CONSCIOUSNESS

The cash-and-respectability nexus into which the labourers of Alleppey entered slightly towards the turn of the nineteenth century, did not, however, automatically mean a much better life in a material sense. The economic power of the Ezhavas increased as long as the market value of their labour did the same, but in general the distribution of the national product of Travancore was no more equitable than in the mid-1800s.

Income differences were very high during the second half of the nineteenth century. While in 1875 the Commercial Agent in Alleppey drew a salary of Rs. 1,000 a month (RAT 1874-5, 1976: 56), the lowest grade government officials (sweepers, etc.), had to live on Rs. 2 a month, and Indian head-clerks on Rs. 12. Coolies and agricultural labourers earned at that time about four *anna*s (one quarter of a rupee) a day plus a meal (Jeffrey 176: 91-2), or even less: five *chackrams* (28½ *chackram*s equal one rupee) is also mentioned (Government of Kerala, 1975: 345). In case of unlikely full employment in terms of working days per month, a monthly wage of Rs. 5 to 6 was then possible, but it was probably actually much less. In order to relate these income figures to data pertaining to costs of living, a survey conducted at Cochin in 1891 is useful. This survey revealed that a man needed Rs. 42 a year to cover his costs of living, while women and children could do with Rs. 29.50. Thus three and a half to two and a half per capita per month, say Rs. 15 for a modest family were required. It is no wonder then that government jobs were sought after, as Jeffrey remarks: an average one would bring in Rs. six to seven a month (Jeffrey, 1976: 105).

Half a century later, in the early 1930s, top salaries were still about Rs. 1,000 a month. Junior clerks and skilled artisans earned Rs. 10 to Rs. 15, and labourers up to Rs. 10, under condition of full employment. Thus: lower incomes were raised compared to the data of 1875. However, it was estimated that an average sized household needed Rs. 20 to Rs. 25 a month to live modestly, and thus several wage earners per household were required among labourers and minor clerks.[7]

However, as long as the work and the products of the Ezhavas in and around Alleppey were in demand by entrepreneurs, the coir workers were in a relatively comfortable position: they became workers, better rewarded than ever, though poor. Emancipatory processes together with demands for better material and working conditions resulted in the formation of trade unions.

Labour Organizations and Labour Struggles

In 1922 a union of labourers was started in Alleppey, the Travancore Labour Association (TLA).[8] The TLA was the first union in Travancore, and a rather early union on an all-India scale. Its start was organized by coir workers who were predominantly of the Ezhava community. The TLA was in that manner an outgrowth of the earlier Ezhava welfare organization, and it functioned in its early period, as Heller describes, as a '. . . caste association, providing "social uplift" and education through reading rooms, night school, welfare schemes, and an ayurvedic hospital' (1999: 171). The caste orientation lost its importance soon after, and a class-orientation emerged.

Heller quotes a clear declaration by the vice-president: 'all workers, whatever be their caste or religion are basically workers. All workers have the same work, same wages and same working time' (Heller, 1999: 171-2).

Other unions followed quickly, and it was in line with these developments that the emerging horizontally based interest organizations of labourers were matched by similar organizations uniting employers. An early organization, the Travancore Chamber of Commerce, started in 1929, brought especially the export-oriented business and manufacturing companies together (after an abortive attempt as early as the 1890s, see Jeffrey, 1984: 1159). Others followed in the 1930s, and united mats and matting manufacturers, oil millers and many others. All together, since the 1920s two 'classes' manifested themselves in the social structure of Alleppey. The process of social mobility in the context of gradual de-feudalization of economy and society resulted hence in a class-like struggle which became increasingly manifest during the 1930s. Though there were also 'peaceful years',[9] labour relations became tense and in the late 1930s these two classes clashed most dramatically during a general strike in 1938. This strike was partly 'traditionally' directed against successive wage cuts in industries during the depression of the 1930s.

Due to falling world market prices, wages in the coir industry were from time to time cut since the late 1920s. For some parts, these cuts were made good by lower food prices as well, but the real wages in the coir industry declined. The industry as such did not suffer from the depression of the 1930s: on the contrary, one might say, its poverty-base was rather more developed (see Chapter 3). Workers protested however with reason to their cuts in wages (Jeffrey, 1984: 1159), and their economic grievances became subject to official enquiries into the coir industry after the ending of the strike.

The strike of 1938 was also directed against the political structure of the state.[10] And partly it went much beyond this, as the capitalist social system was attacked ('Destroy Capitalism' was a slogan, Jeffrey, 1984). The strike resulted also in a split between a more moderate wing of the labour movement and a more radical one, eventually resulting in strongholds for either the Congress movement, or the communist parties in independent Kerala.[11]

In retrospect, this period of the social and political history of Travancore, in which the workers and the employers of Alleppey can be seen as trendsetters within the state, has been commented upon at length and in an apologetic manner towards Travancore's labourers in the report of the Census of 1941, of which a part is cited here:

> The relation between employer and employee has been more cordial in agriculture than in industrial economy. . . . The industrial operative . . . is treated by his employer more like an automaton functioning as an economic unit in his moneymaking concern, without the sentimental attachments to the master, noticeable among the agricultural tenants. . . . In organized industries the reciprocity of those who offer and accept service is determined by what Carlyle calls 'the cash-nexus'. The absence of cultural contacts between the employer and employee has unfortunately led to a clash of interests resulting in the demand for protective organizations to safeguard each other's rights. This tendency has led to the rise of Trade Unionism in all industrial countries and internationalization in recent years. Capitalist obduracy against the claims of labour organizations has forced the latter in some Western countries to adopt the programme of direct action through strikes, etc. and thereby set on foot the Syndicalist movement tending towards socialism that advocated the destruction of capitalism by the nationalisation of all wealth. . . . The incipient character of organized industry in Travancore has taken it no further than the frontiers and the outskirts of such problems. . . . For one thing, the employer started business on terms reasonable enough to preclude any palpable disability. Factories and estates in the initial stages being few and far between, the operatives had little occasion to be detrimentally affected by the rigours and restrictions to which the pressures of competition might have forced their employers to subject them. When the prospect of large-scale business and joint stock concerns became manifest to local producers more factories were set up and keen business

> competition set in, which prejudicially affected the business and ultimately the wage-rates. As long as the various factories and estates were based on stable capital and sound organization, the pernicious effects of competition were not so intense or widespread as to result in agitation. But when numerous mushroom concerns cropped up with little capital and less organization, competition became unbridled, often of the cutthroat type, and constrained the employers to tighten their purse strings and stiffen their attitudes to their operatives, who thereupon sought to safeguard their interest by starting labour unions which gave them greater strength. (Census of India 1941-I, 1942: 97)

Despite the gradually mounting tensions to which the 1941-Census reporter referred, it cannot be said that entrepreneurs opposed trade unionism as such. They acknowledged in general the right of organization of labourers provided these organizations aimed at the promotion of labourers' interests within the *status quo* of a liberal and capitalist export-oriented economy. One might add that the social transformation from slaves and downtrodden was not inconvenient to entrepreneurs. There was no need for them anymore to be patrons and exploit slaves: they could just become capitalist entrepreneurs owning or managing capitalist firms and thus owning or managing capital and hiring labour.

However, as is mentioned in Chapter 4, the economy of Alleppey, at least during the 1920s, was expanding and as long as profits rose, there was some bargaining left for both parties: probably a small amount for labourers and still a sizeable amount for entrepreneurs.

New Keralese Realities

The strike of 1938 also yielded a structural radicalization among Alleppey's working population. The Congress movement, which started to support the workers, betrayed them in the end whereupon a Communist Party was created in Alleppey (see Jeffrey, 1984: 1163). This party has become a decisive factor in state politics since the 1950s, together with the split-off Communist Party of India (Marxist) in 1964.

Jeffrey could therefore conclude his analysis of the coir workers movement in the 1930s with the word 'The coir unions have been bastions of support for one Communist Party or another to this day' (1984: 1163).

Until the 1950s, the process of structural change in Alleppey's society remained largely latent in terms of change in the real and ultimate structure of local power. The commitment by the State of Travancore to the business interest of the (foreign) entrepreneurs was firm enough to guarantee that no challenges to those interests were allowed beyond a certain limit. That limit was the social order of capitalism itself. When trade unions rallied around more radical demands, such as the call to destroy capitalism, the state power and the economic elites took to outspoken and harsh repression. The Travancore government, for example, did not hesitate—even in 1946—to employ its armed forces against a 'leftist uprising' in and around Alleppey, at the cost of many hundred of lives (Kusuman, 1977).

But after Independence and the subsequent merger of Travancore within India, the challenge to the power structure of the society of Alleppey and that of Travancore transformed itself from a latent into a manifest reality. The newly emerging Indian Union, the formation of Kerala out of Travancore, Cochin, and Malabar district of the former Madras Province; and the take over of Kerala's state government by left-wing political parties (in 1957) paved the way for trade unions to have a real say in the economic life of the town. Labour demands were honoured by entrepreneurs instead of being challenged (see e.g. Lieten, 1980; Isaac, 1982), while the foreign entrepreneurs became suspected characters rather than the 'pillars of society' as they used to be seen by the Travancore state administration.

It is one of the bitter contradictions of this stage of the process of changing social relations that a firmer grip on the local economy by workers was accompanied by a rapidly declining amount of work. The more the labourers managed to get a better share of the 'gross urban product', the more this product shrank. The number of jobs declined, while the transfer from well protected jobs in industries falling under the Factory Act (such as the large-scale coir manufacturing units) towards jobs in the small-scale and household-scale coir processing units, where labour conditions were much worse and wages much lower, led to a substantial decline in the standard of living among very many workers in Alleppey. Labour organizations tried to counter this trend by the creation of cooperative coir production societies, but these never made a sizeable impact on the structure of coir manufacturing in Alleppey (see Isaac, 1982; Schampers, 1984). A picture emerges of powerful labour unions with only a few powerful labourers and many underemployed and unemployed 'back-benchers'. Few labourers eventually found work in the 'organized coir sector' and had their interest protected by trade unions and labour legislation. For many, trade union and political party protection has become hollow, leaving many workers with the gains of a lengthy process from downtrodden castes to conscious workers, but without jobs.

NOTES

1. Jeffrey gives—besides a wealth of data on nineteenth-century Travancore—a comprehensive overview of the main case and caste-like groupings in his book of 1976 (pp. 9-26). Further there are various anthropological, sociological, historical, and other publications on the peculiar Keralese system of castes and primordial social relations, as well as on specific castes.
2. Actually, for this group of 'soil slaves' the more appropriate term seems to be serfdom, attached as the 'slaves' were to the soil, rather than to the master. The term slavery, however, is most widely used (se also RRSC-I: 56-9, and for more details, Kusuman 1973).
3. To avoid any misunderstandings about the role of the missionaries, let me quote Jeffrey (1976: 38): 'Did the European missionaries come to Travancore with the intention of uplifting the low castes? The answer is emphatically no. They came to make converts and

save souls. But like strangers at a party where they were snubbed by half the guests, they were too bewildered to offer much resistance when the other half took them by the arm and led them into a corner. The missionaries were spurrned by the high castes and monopolized by the low'. N.K. Bhaskaran is slightly more empathic. He agrees with Jeffrey regarding the ultimate goal of the missionary societies, but he added that: 'The pitiable plight of the low castes genuinely moved many Christian missionaries' (1984: 210).

4. In some respects only! Caste ascription has persisted over a long time in Travancore as elsewhere in India, and it still persists in many societal aspects. In this respect it can hardly be expected that the effects of the abolition of slavery in the 1850s were overwhelming. 'In a society ridden by caste prejudice, it was not surprising that this proclamation (of 1854, HS) became utterly inoperative', is concluded by the RRSC-I, 1970: 58).
5. See for the complex and unclear history of the Ezhavas in Travancore, and their position as an 'untouchable', or 'depressed' community the convenient description of Ouwerkerk 1994, chapter II.
6. The Ezhavas as a caste can be called the most important exponent of the transfer from feudality to (some) commercialization and capitalism, from ascribed to (somewhat) achieved status.
7. The data of the 1930s are based on oral information (see Chapter 8). See also Census of India 1931, 1932.
8. The union originated from the SNDP caste welfare organization of the Ezhava caste. Its start is described by A.O. Ouwerkerk, 1994: 63-4; and Heller, 1999: 171 ff.)
9. From a communication with the Swiss firm Volkart Brothers, specialized in the manufacture and shipping of ropes for the European vineyards.
10. A responsible government was demanded, instead of the autocratic regime of the maharaja.
11. See Heller (1999) for an account of the labour movement and its political translation.

CHAPTER 6

Space and Society: Social Aspects of Alleppey's Spatial Development

THE SOCIO-SPATIAL DEVELOPMENT OF EARLY ALLEPPEY

In preceding chapters, the technical, economic, political and social dimensions of the start and the subsequent growth of Alleppey have been discussed. In this chapter the occupation of space of the new town, and its societal meaning take a central position. Until 1762, the hamlet Alappuzha at the dead end of a small stream on the Western outskirts of the backwaters, seemed the only inhabited place in the area where Alleppey was to be built. The hamlet consisted probably of a few Konkani traders and some artisans, among them apparently some blacksmiths who, according to one interpretation, coined the name of the settlement. While the artisans lived along the stream, the Konkani merchants occupied an area directly north of it: Tirumala. The Konkani had a temple in that area, while in the south of present-day Alleppey another temple existed where Kesava Das used to stay when visiting his new port-under-construction. The site before 1762 is given in a rough sketch (Figure 6.1).

What was done from 1762 onwards was extremely simple and straightforward in view of the objectives of the government of Travancore. A canal was dug—or rather extended—from the Alappuzha hamlet and stream to the beach in order to bring merchandize by boat close to the sea, while on its banks godowns and an office of the state Commercial Department (Cutcherry) were built. These were actually the

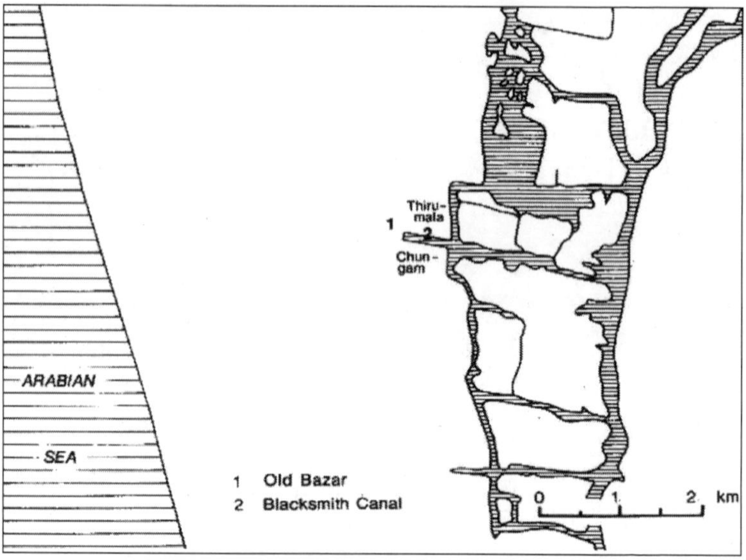

Figure 6.1: Alapuzha before 1762.
Sketchmap drawn by Hans Schenk/Jan ter Haar
(University of Amsterdam).

main public works conducted in Alleppey. Along the banks of the canal—Commercial Canal—the traders who were invited by minister Kesava Das settled as a community. Muslims stayed south of the canal, Christians north of it, while Hindus lived on both sides, though there was some segregation according to caste. The Konkani Brahmins had their nucleus in the east, in Tirumala, and later also near the palace of the *maharaja* in the south-east. Kerala Brahmins, like the Namboodiris, stayed west of Tirumala around the area where the temple and the street named Mulakkal is now. Gujaratis—possibly including Kutchis and Sindhis, Parsis and members of the Bania community, concentrated in the west, where there is even now a Gujarati Street. In Figure 6.2 this original pattern has been given. It did not undergo many changes afterwards, though some diffusion has occurred. However, the pattern of community segregation is much less marked than in many other Indian towns. No distinct cast *falia*s, or *wadi*s can be discerned.

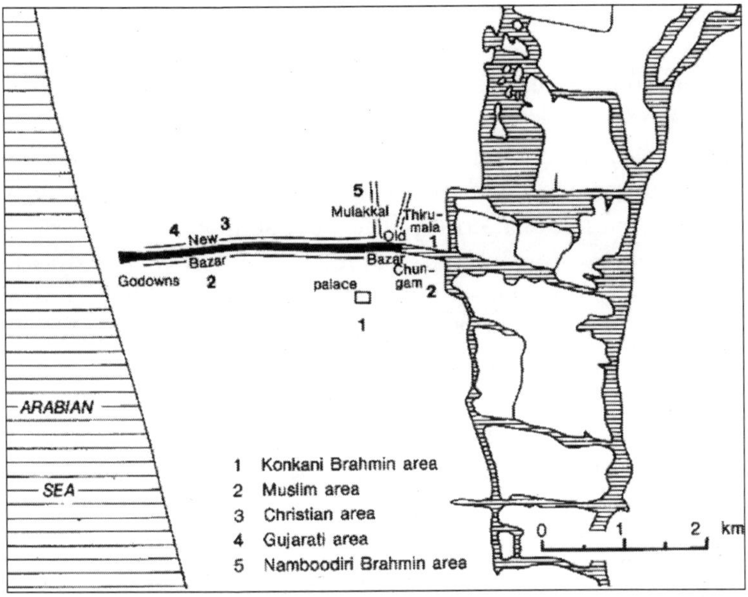

Figure 6.2: Alleppey: Planned developments in the 1700s. Sketchmap drawn by Hans Schenk/Jan ter Haar (University of Amsterdam).

This description seems rather obvious in view of the physical characteristics of the region around Alleppey (see Chapter 3) and its social structure. The occupation of the created space which came to be known as Alleppey can be given a wider significance when the social meaning of the occupied space is considered. This will be done in the next section.

COMMERCIAL CANAL: SYMBOL AND FUNCTION

Several authors dealing with urban history in India have stressed the relation between dominant urban social structures and the use of urban space. Lewandowski, for example (1977, 1979), who analysed two cities in Tamil Nadu (Madurai and Madras—now Chennai) sees the use of the urban space in Madurai as a reflection of its 'ceremonial' function, whereby sacred and secular power in combination superseded that of trade and commerce and has become visible in the absolute temple complex in the heart of the town (1977; 1979; see also Ramesh & Noble, 1977). In early Madras, the dominance of political power combined with economic power exercised by the EIC was expressed in the factory-cum-fort complex as a visual and functional core of the early settlement and was its symbol. In a more recent article, Lewandowski has drawn attention to the post-colonial use of space in Madras as a means to deliberately manipulate the built environment in order to legitimate Tamil politics (1983).

Fonseca has stressed the logic of the 'indigenous cities' in north India by analysing—explaining almost—the solid relationships between the urban society of Shahjahanabad (Delhi) and its urban form (1969). He argues in strong wording the logic of the spatial structure of the *bazar*s including the fine-grained interplay of *mohalla*s and *chowk*s and connecting routes, as reflecting similarly fine-grained social and economic relations and values regarding working and living. King shows extensively and convincingly that the spatial symbolic values of the colonial urban spatial structure are closely related to its culture, its technology and its power. Thus, spacious bungalows, segregation of urban functions, long distances, segregation of classes and ethnic groups characterized New Delhi. The residence of the viceroy combined both societal ranking systems and spatial eminence and symbolized a 'temple of imperial power' (King, 1976: 239).

By looking at eighteenth-century Alleppey, as it was constructed purposefully, one might accordingly look for a dominant spatial form, expressing and symbolizing the early character of the new state trading settlement. No temple, no mosque was built to symbolize Alleppey's character. They were built, but modestly and not at central locations. Nor was there a palace to perform a symbolic function. The palace built after 1762 was almost hidden and was far beyond Alleppey's sites of economic activities: Travancore's formal political power was thus hardly physically present. The office of actual power, the commercial department—at the beach—was more prominently located.

No *bazar* was built to demonstrate the close relation between working and living, possibly also due to the absence of a sizeable retail trade and artisan tradition in Travancore. The sites known as 'Old Bazar' (near the Allappuzha hamlet) and 'New Bazar' (along the south bank of Commercial Canal not far from the beach; see Figure 6.2, were 'shopping streets', not resembling north Indian *bazar*s, as Fonseca described them: a densely packed mixture of artisan-based production, storage and services (1969: 107-8; see also Dutt, 1983). The only dominant spatial expression of the character of Alleppey as it developed from 1762 onwards, is its main canal—Commercial Canal. This canal was the lifeline of the town and the very heart of it. Commercial Canal was the main, and almost only transport artery, and on its banks godowns, business offices, residences of traders and similar building were constructed.

The symbolic value of Commercial Canal culminated at its dead end—a few hundred meters from the sea—where it widens somewhat to make for more manoeuvring space for the *vellam*, and where godowns were concentrated. Moreover, the *cutcherry* and (later), the light house, the pier, the residence of the Commercial Agent and the seat of the Roman Catholic Bishop were to be found there. Still later, the offices and residences of the European entrepreneurs were found along the canal and close to the beach, while the main coir factories were established slightly more to the east. Gujarati Street was close to the beach too; it ran from Commercial Canal to the north and showed the importance of the north Indian trading communities in the original social structure of the town.

Commercial Canal was the symbol of early Alleppey on its own merit and due to the absence of any other symbol. The canal accentuated Alleppey as a trading and transporting town. Moreover, its pre-eminence was given additional strength by the absence of forts, temples, mosques, palaces and *mohalla*s as potential focal points. Forts were considered unnecessary all through Alleppey's history, while temples and palaces were considered of minor importance, as has been noted above. What mattered was trade and transport: hence the artery of trade and transport, the canal and its embankments, could not be anything but the virtual core and symbol of the early town as a centre of wholesale trade and shipment.

Physical planning in the nineteenth and early twentieth centuries included the digging of a parallel canal (Vadai Canal) 4 furlongs north of Commercial Canal. Two short canals connected the main canals in the western and the eastern sections of the town while the area between the canals were spatially 'filled in' by a regular chequer-board type road pattern (Figure 6.3). Later, the built-up urban space gradual expanded north and south of the two canals.

As the character of Alleppey changed from its trade dominance to an industrial settlement, Commercial Canal kept its central role in the urban economy, assisted by Vadai Canal. Commercial Canal carried the *vellam* from the backwater villages to the factories along its banks. There, small jetties, quays and stairs bear witness to the transhipment of coir yarn

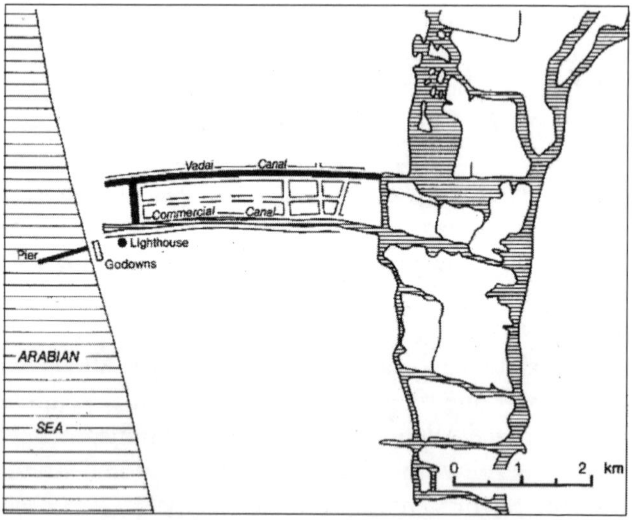

Figure 6.3: Extensions during the 1800s.
Sketchmap drawn by Hans Schenk/Jan ter Haar
(University of Amsterdam).

from the small boats to the factory premises of William Goodacre, Darragh Samil, Aspinwall and so many other companies. From there occasional roads to the north and the south brought workers from the outskirts and from surrounding villages to the factories. Tens of thousands of them: old residents liked to recall from the 1920s and 1930s the dense crowds on the banks and on the bridges in the evening: '. . . one could walk on the heads of the people', they said. Commercial Canal, together with the long, low whitewashed walls of the coir factories facing the waterfront, symbolized Alleppey again in its years of economic prosperity. And again, no other landmark could challenge the canal. No *bazar* emerged in spite of names and in spite of the many thousands passing through New Bazar, or shopping in the market more or les opposite New Bazar and slightly beyond the houses on the northern bank.[1] The market remained hidden by the waterfront structures and New Bazar just added to the dominance of Commercial Canal: that shallow, filthy, dark stretch of water, home of rats, bearer of diseases, open gutter, but crowded with *vellam*, at the time in 'an endless arrival and departure of canoes loaden with merchandise' (Pillai, 1940: 115), flanked with crowds and obviously the *sine qua non* of Alleppey.

The downfall of the economic base of Alleppey brought decay to the town and this had become most visible at Commercial Canal and its immediate surroundings in the late 1970s.[2] The jetties, quays and stairs were broken and overgrown with weed. A few rusty cranes leant over the water in which they were not mirrored as it was filled with floating weeds: 'African-Weed' (Salvinia). Some of the coir godowns and factories have almost collapsed and so are the proud headquarters of the coir manufacturing and trading companies.' The coir business has for a great deal retreated from Commercial Canal, as could also be seen at New Bazar. Elsewhere in the town new activities have sprung up and the bridges over Commercial Canal merely connects other areas of attraction, instead of its two banks. Yet, Commercial Canal remained the symbolic heart of Alleppey, even though it became obsolete and rather useless. It sadly marks Alleppey's past. It provided for the 'unexpected' when one approached it: the sudden sight of a waterway, going from nowhere to nearly nowhere, carrying only some *vellam*, loaded with bricks or sand; a rubbish dump, but yet unrivalled in its symbolic power.

A few areas in the town now perform central services for its inhabitants: a food market north of Commercial Canal, a concentration of financial institutions, mainly south of it. Mullakkal, the street that connects Vadai Canal with Commercial Canal in the east side of the town, is the most outstanding retail centre for non-food products, such as jewellery, electrical fittings, textiles, etc, while on the eastern outskirts the processing and trade of copra, coconut oil is concentrated in Chungam, a busy part of the city. If, however, an inhabitant of Alleppey would in, say, 1980 be asked to locate the urban centre, he or she would probably mention Mullakkal. This street is somewhat besides the main traffic arteries and resembles a pedestrian precinct. It is exactly that for many citizens, a favourite place for 'being in town', for meeting friends, strolling around, shopping perhaps, or having a drink in the Indian Coffee House.

Figure 6.4: Commercial Canal (Photograph by Hans Schenk).

Commercial Canal, just at the southern tip of Mullakkal, continues however, to visualize the lifeline of an earlier economy, as if it has become an open-air museum of industrial and transport technology in its many early decades.

POPULATION: NUMBERS AND SETTLEMENT PATTERNS

The municipal area of Alleppey grew gradually in size, mainly north and south of its canals. It is however difficult to make sound statements on this size and the number of people living in a designated area, at least before the twentieth century, as the following, slightly bewildering overview might show.

The urban limits before 1921 were inconsistently defined. The limits of Alleppey were defined for the first time for census reason in 1891. They were defined by compiling a number of *karas*—'natural villages'—or neighbourhoods. These *karas* had no demarcated limits. For the 1891 census, a number of *karas* were *ad hoc* named 'Alleppey' and their population totals added together. Thus, areas such as 'Alleppey South of the Palace Road' and 'East of Alleppey Jail' were combined (Census of Travancore, 1891-II, 1894: 1036-7). From 1901 the basic unit of counting became the 'revenue village'. In 1901 that was the *proverti*, a rather large unit, not necessarily coinciding with (a number of) *karas*. From 1911 onwards the *proverti* was changed for the much smaller *pakuthi* as a new revenue unit and also as a basic counting unit for census purposes. However, neither *provertis* nor *pakuthis* necessarily coincided with the demarcation of the concept of 'census town',[3] and even now there exists a revenue village Alleppey which is partly beyond the limits of the municipal town, i.e. a settlement with a local governing body. Problems in assessing the urban population were unavoidable: nature of revenue units had to be divided into municipal and non-municipal areas.

I have mentioned in Chapter 3 that it was estimated that Alleppey (however delimitated) counted in the 1860s less that 15,000 inhabitants. This number appears to have risen to almost 23,000 at the above-mentioned Travancore census and almost 26,000 ten years later at the Census of India. The inhabitants lived in an area of 3.54 sq. mile (9.17 sq. km) in a rectangle of about 4.5 km east to west (that is: from the backwaters to the beach) and some 2 km north to south, 1 km south of Commercial Canal and a few hundred meters north of Vadai Canal. The limits of the census town were a bit stretched for the 1921 census and coincided henceforth with the municipal borders. This meant a population increase till about 32,000 inhabitants. It appears, however, that this expanded municipality of 1921 had a population density that was more or less equal to that of earlier decades: 2,713 per sq. km in 1901, 2,799 in 1911 and 2,727 in the larger area in 2021. Apparently the rural stretches north and south of Alleppey were as densely inhabited as the town.[4]

This observation corresponds to several similar ones on the pattern of the rural and urban settlements in Kerala. Woodcock (1967), Ansari (1969), Unni (1969) and others mention the narrow margin between town and countryside in physical terms. Woodcock describes Kerala's villages as 'half-urbanised' and its towns as 'half-rural' (1967: 44-9). In the 1931 Census report it was remarked that 'Towns are only out-grown villages' (Census of India 1931, vol. XXVIII-I, 1932: 129), while ten years later it was observed that hard and fast lines between towns and villages were not easy to draw, towns being at best 'out-grown' villages with additional amenities and facilities for commerce and communication (Census of India 1941, vol. XXV-I, 1942: 25). This pattern has continued. Jesbin Skariah Thomas remarked on basis of 2011 census data that: 'The special characteristics of Kerala are that one cannot identify the rural-urban disparity as visually seen in other states' (2019: 26).

A rather reliable reconstruction of the historical pattern of the use of space of the area which has now become Alleppey confirms the earlier assumption that Alleppey's start was very much that of a 'business district'. Some traders lived in the early developed zone, alongside or close to Commercial Canal, but the canal area was mainly meant for entrepreneurial purposes. Gradually residential developments took place, but the bulk of labour lived beyond the canal area and travelled or commuted from within the urban boundaries but increasingly from beyond these boundaries to their places of work in the business area. In the report of the 1931 Census it has been formulated that:

> Daily migration is now a common feature of important towns like Trivandrum, Nagercoil, Quilon and Alleppey. A number of people live outside the town, go there to work in the morning and return home in the evening. (vol. XXVIII, 1932: 86)

The surrounding villages have actually 'fed' Alleppey. Ever since the urban limits were drawn and redrawn, more villages and parts of villages were included in the census town and municipal town and thus augmented to the subsequent urban population totals. This process was admitted in the report of the 1951 census: 'The increase of 106 per cent of the population of Alleppey during the last decade[5] is not an increase in population with urban traits' (Census of India 1951, 1953, vol. XIII: 38). This growth of the population north and south of Alleppey's core—both within the municipal borders and beyond was largely natural. There was no sizeable stream of in-migrants from elsewhere. This was already noticed in a more general manner in the 1911 Census report: 'The tendency to migrate, whether within the state or outside it, is as present only a tendency and a weak one too' (Census of India 1911, 1912, vol. XIII, Travancore: 68). Later census reports do not stress in or out-migration.

The occupation of residential space in the Alleppey region can thus be considered as extraordinarily simple. All throughout the history of the town it has been mainly based on a sedentary pattern of growth: population increase on the spot. This growth led to a gradual expansion of town and villages, whereby these villages around Alleppey which functioned to a fair degree as a labour reservoir, and as commuter homesteads, became urban wards and continued to function in this manner. To some extent this process is still going on. A map of the distribution of the urban population in 1971, shows a remarkable equal pattern of densities per ward, apart from two eastern wards: backwater areas incorporated in the town (see Figure 6.5 and Appendix, Table 5).[6] Population increases are still partly met by clearing parts of the 'jungle' even right within Alleppey, and partly by the 'filling in' of still spacious compounds with gradually more and more new huts and houses.[7] There are some accents, though, in this equal pattern. Industrial workers tend to live in the north-western wards of the town, according to the 1971 census, and workers on the transport sectors, in the southern wards.

The wards do not look overcrowded. Vast hutment areas—so visible in many Indian towns and cities—cannot be found in Alleppey. There are a couple of small clusters of huts, but not in any way as extensive and numerous as is common

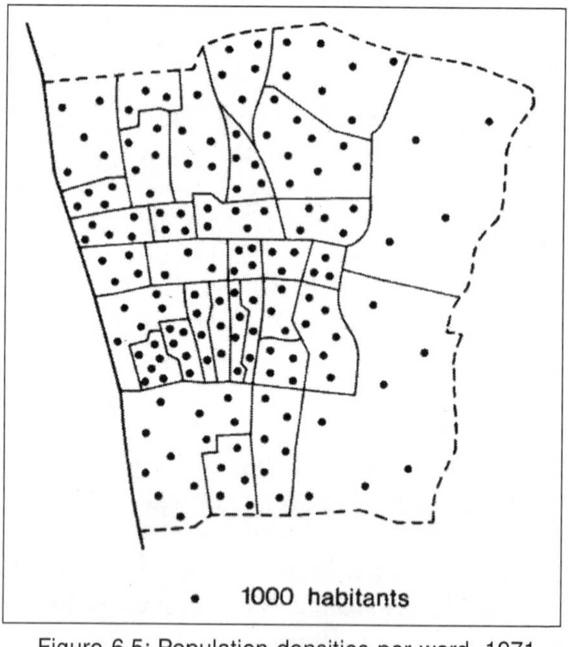

Figure 6.5: Population densities per ward, 1971, based on Appendix Table 5. Sketchmap drawn by Hans Schenk/Jan ter Haar (University of Amsterdam).

elsewhere in India. Huts are made of bamboo, mats and palm leaves and their construction is often very poor, denying any comfort to their inhabitants. In most parts of the town, they stand isolated, in small compounds, hidden behind banana plants and shadowed by coconut trees. Many poor citizens own small pieces of land to build their huts under the *kudikadappu* scheme of land distribution to the landless during the 1960s. Most plots do not exceed 5 or 6 cents[8], but they provide for a certain privacy, and space to dig a latrine, to build a 'bathroom' from a few mats and poles, to grow some fruits or some *chira-ila* and other vegetables. Many compounds are fenced by shrubs and cactuses, large ones may include small ponds.

Overcrowding is however there, write Schampers regarding the ward where he did research in 1978-80:

> when looking at the density per house/hut. There were 234 one room house/huts giving space to 1,367 persons. This meant an average of 5.8 persons per one room house/hut. There were 485 two room houses/ huts giving space to 2,826 persons. This meant an average of 2.9 persons per room. (1984: 53)

This picture holds true for many areas in Alleppey.

Yet, the urban scenery is often beautiful as well as treacherous. 'When coconuts abound, there cannot be underemployment', exclaimed Hatch when visiting Travancore in the 1930s (1933: 23). However, one should rather say: the coconut tree hides unemployment and poverty. Its nuts are often pledged as security with a bank or a moneylender, and so are even its leaves. It only provides some shadow and an un-Indian townscape.

NOTES

1. Even in a more recent description of the shape of Alleppey in preparation for a development plan for the town, it is written that: 'the commercial and business areas of Alleppey, generally can be said to be lacking in compactness and cohesion' (Government of Kerala, 1966: 35).

2. Data in these sections are taken with permission from an unpublished economic census, undertaken by the Alleppey branch of the State Bureau of Economics and Statistics, unless mentioned otherwise.
3. A census town is defined as a settlement with over 5,000 inhabitants. More than 75 per cent of its male working population should find employment outside the agricultural sector, while the density should be over four hundred persons/sq. km.
4. Densities declined considerably when the municipal (and census-town) borders were substantially redrawn by the inclusion of large sparsely inhabited stretches of the backwaters into Alleppey in 1951 and 1961.
5. In the 1941 Census 56,333 residents have been counted, in the census of 1952: 116,278.
6. These data are taken from the Census of India 1971(series 9), 1973.
7. Even now this 'jungle' is prominently visible in many places in the town. It gives shelter to some of its original inhabitants such as poisonous snakes. In a small hutment area nearby our house, about one person died each month from snake bites during the period of our stay in 1979. In our compound a huge snake lived in an enclosed corner. It was left in peace by our landlord as it was considered harmless.
8. In metric terms this come to about 10 to 12 by 20 m.

CHAPTER 7

Public Health and the Emergence of Local Government in Alleppey

EARLY LOCAL GOVERNMENT IN ALLEPPEY

Since 1762 the dominant local power in Alleppey, both in a political and in an economic sense, was vested in the Commercial Department of the state and its Commercial Agent in-charge of this department. Since the early 1800s a Briton held this position of head of the Commercial Department (see Chapter 1). This department controlled the main state monopolies of its export trade till the 1860s, though some minor monopolies were maintained. The Commercial Agent dealt also with the activities in the port with regard to trade. Moreover, the Commercial Agent was not only in-charge of the port and its related activities, but also of the few public institutions, notably those for maintaining law and order. In the Report of the Administration of Travancore for the year 1877/78 his full responsibilities are specified as such:

> In his commercial activity, he serves as the medium of purchases from and sales in foreign markets of various foreign commodities required by the state and such indigenous forest products of government monopoly as timber, ivory, cardamoms, etc., respectively and exercises supervision over the bonded warehouses for tobacco as well as over the importation, storage and distribution of Bombay salt. He is also ex officio the local Master Attendant, Police Superintendent, Magistrate, Conservancy Officer, Special Magistrate and Justice of the Peace. (RAT1877-8: 115)

In each of these capacities he advised the government or had executive powers to act. For example, he advised the Public Works Department of the state to deepen the canals of Alleppey, as these fell under the authority of that department, for the purpose of transport but also for reasons of public health. A Commercial Agent is quoted in the annual administration report of the next year:

> I would strongly recommend the Wada Canal being deepened and a short canal being made to join the main and the Wada. This would stop the overcrowding and create a current which would help both canals from getting foul. (RAT 1878-9: 111).

The responsibilities of the Commercial Agent in Alleppey were exceptional in Travancore. Local affairs elsewhere used to be looked after by the local police force, controlled by the Division *peishkar*s and their *taluk tahsildar*s[1] (see Government of Kerala 1975: 440). It was only in Alleppey that these affairs were in-charge beyond the authority of the Police Department of the state, but within that of the Commercial Department. The situation in Alleppey shows also that there was no clear watershed demarcation between the administration of the port and that of the town. It becomes, moreover clear that concern about public health, increasingly important all over both the Princely states and the British possessions on the subcontinent from the early 1800s onwards, was not a prominent issue in Travancore.

In many urban places of the subcontinent have initiatives been noted, directed at the improvement of sanitation and related public works, since the early decades of the nineteenth century. Often such measures originated in the gradual neglect by the East India Company of traditionally existing urban public health measures, and hence the rising sanitary problems, notably in the ever denser built-up slums and hutment areas. Such initiatives were taken by concerned British and Indian citizens and were incidentally supported by public authorities in one way or the other. Some initiatives led to more permanent semi-official local urban committees, though other ones were short-lived. Increasing sanitary dangers; increasing feelings of uneasiness among the rising number of British residents as well as Indian elites in—notably—the core settlements of the EIC (Calcutta, Madras, Bombay) but also in major cities along the Ganges and elsewhere; increasing desires among the urban elites to secure 'a minimum standard of health and comfort' (Harrison 1980: 172) led from the middle of the nineteenth century to the demand for institutionalized 'modern' local government. It led simultaneously to the desire to take part in local government, initially on a restricted basis ('taxpayers', representatives of 'interest groups' and the like), later, in the twentieth century on a universal scale).[2] Town Improvement Committees were often the resulting institutionalized answers to the perceived public health dangers.

It was not before 1894 that Travancore installed Town Improvement Committees (TIC) in four so-called Conservancy Towns, including Alleppey. There is no doubt that this installation was motivated by the wish to improve the public hygiene and related matters. The State Town Fund backing the TICs should be spent 'on the supervision of sanitary arrangements' as it was stated in retrospective overview of the TIC-period in Travancore (TAR 1928-9: 234). This meant also that henceforth local citizens could in a structural way participate in local affairs.

THE TOWN IMPROVEMENT COMMITTEE OF ALLEPPEY: AN OUTLINE

Travancore's four Town Improvement Committees consisted of only nominated members by the state government , five to nine in total. The committee in Alleppey counted seven members. In all other towns 'officials' (civil servants) outnumbered non-official members. In Alleppey, however non-official members formed a majority in the committee.[3] The president of the TIC's used to be the Division *peishkar*, except again in Alleppey, where the Commercial Agent was nominated as such, underlining once more the special position of the town within the administration of Travancore. The TICs in Travancore existed from 1894 till 1920, when they were transformed into municipal councils. During this quarter of a century, the committees gradually expanded and cemented their position in the local society.

In Alleppey, membership increased to nine in 1903-4. Moreover, the non-official members became gradually elected members, chosen by and from the ratepayers of the town, according to Rules, enacted in 1911-12. In Alleppey four such non-official members (a minority in the committee) were elected from 1911-12 onwards, while one year later all non-official members were given the privilege of being elected, as it was put in the RAT for the year 1913-14 (p. 53). In 1915-16 again three non-official members were added to the TIC of Alleppey, but two of these members were nominated in order to: 'safeguard the interests of the unrepresented minorities' (RAT 1916-17: 61). Four years later all TICs of Travancore were succeeded by fully elected councils, and the intermediate era of local government in Travancore and in Alleppey came to an end.

ALLEPPEY'S TIC IN ACTION: EXAMPLES DURING ITS EARLY YEARS

What has been mentioned in the annual reports of the state government about its TICs? Examples of activities taken by the TIC of Alleppey or by state agencies during the early years after its installation are given below, in order to get an idea what went on in the office of the TIC and in the town. Concern of the TIC for the public health of Alleppey encompassed a wide range of public health dimensions. This concern included the provision of drinking water, the introduction of a system of scavenging and sweeping, the removal of certain activities that were considered dangerous to the public from certain sites, and the preventive vaccinations against cholera and smallpox, etc. But what did this mean in the daily work of the committee? The staff pattern of

Alleppey's TIC in its first year gives some idea what could in practice be expected from the committee. Its staff consisted in 1894-5 of forty-one persons, out of which thirty-four were sweepers, in addition to an inspector, an assistant-inspector, a sub-overseer, a clerk and three peons. In another conservancy town in Travancore were lampmen on the payroll, but not in Alleppey. They came, however in later years. Hence, sweeping seems to have been 'the' major task, despite expressed concerns on other aspects of public health. But some activities were certainly undertaken, as the following examples show. In 1895-6 sites were selected for slaughter houses, fish markets and a hide depot, to reduce the nuisance emanating from them. For the same reasons 'proper ginger bleaching cisterns' were arranged (RAT 1895-6: 127). One year later a system of private scavenging was introduced in Alleppey. At the same time thought was given to the improvement of the drainage system of the town and to provisions for good drinking water (RAT 1897-8).[4] Meanwhile shallow wells and tanks were dug and repaired in later years. The following years were devoted to 'special precautionary measures against plagues' (RAT 1897-8, Part II: 120) and against other epidemic diseases, and not without reason. 'Smallpox raged in a very virulent form during the greater part of the year and special remedial measures were taken, was written in the report of the year 1901-2 (RAT 1901-2: 45). Such measures included the provision of more dustbins and the erection of temporary latrines. In 1903-4 a plague shed was constructed.

Apart from the concern by the TIC for preventive activities in the sphere of public health, the committees had other duties too. The TIC of Alleppey introduced traffic rules for the town in 1895-6 and controlled its implementation. It exercised a marginal land use control, such as in 1895-6 when a recreation ground 'for the use of the public' was opened (RAT 1896-7: 143). Similarly, encroachments were removed from the public roads. The Administrative Report of 1897-8 summarizes the tasks of the TIC of Alleppey adequately:

Besides the usual attention paid to the conservancy and sanitation of the town, much useful work was done towards their general improvement. The works executed by and at the instance of the committee consisted chiefly of sinking and repairing of public wells and tanks, the construction and repairs of roads, drains and latrines and the improvement of town sites and water supply generally. (RAT 1897-8 Part II: 120)

THE NATURE OF ALLEPPEY: EXPLANATIONS FOR RETARDED URBAN LOCAL GOVERNMENT

It is clear from the above that public health was the main concern of Alleppey's TIC, and its functioning can be compared with that of similar committees in other parts of the subcontinent. The question posed earlier can then be repeated: why was it that urban local government was so much later introduced in Alleppey than elsewhere in India? A first answer is that the local elites in Alleppey, the small European colony and Indian elites, almost all traders and industrialists in the course of the nineteenth century, did not need local government. These groups 'ran' the town, were in control over town affairs through the Commercial Department and its head, the British Commercial Agent, as I mentioned above. One may speculate that the representatives of the omnipotent trade interests brought together in Alleppey, could influence (or even stipulate) local matters more efficiently than a civic body as a Town Improvement Committee could do. This situation continued during the twentieth century, when the British-dominated Travancore Chamber of Commerce was actually more powerful than any other local institution (see Chapter 8). Besides, it seems that until the end of the nineteenth century there was probably less need felt by the local elites to be deeply concerned with public hygiene and related matters than in many other towns elsewhere on the subcontinent. Several factors—in combination—can explain this lack of interest. These factors could sometimes be very trivial, but they should not be neglected. The factors can be grouped in two broad categories, the first dealing with the specific environmental qualities of Alleppey, the second with its social structure.

(a) ENVIRONMENTAL QUALITIES

Soil Structure

Unlike elsewhere in the subcontinent, the presence of the alluvial and sandy soils on which Alleppey was built were relatively well suited to absorb the human waste of the low density of habitation prevailing in the town at that time. (This aspect has apparently well taken into consideration, in view of the fact that of the members of two out of every three households had even in 1960 to use 'open land' for the production of human waste, see below.)

Low Densities of Habitation

Compared to the densely inhabited central urban areas in many Indian urban places, the Alleppey townscape was—and is—quite unusual. Right in the central area of the town, compounds were common in which houses were hidden by coconut trees and many other plants and trees (see Chapter 6). The residential areas could be considered as outgrown village-like clusters.

Abundancy of Water

Again, unlike many other towns, Alleppey and other urban places were close to the sea or to the sizeable inland 'backwaters' basin. The backwaters provided for an abundancy of flowing water which could always wash away or absorb dirt, or at least could seem to do so.

(b) THE SOCIAL STRUCTURE: ALLEPPEY AS A FRONTIER TOWN

Though Alleppey definitely formed a link in a chain in a colonial extraction economy during the 1800s, it can also be labelled as a frontier town from the point of view of the European residents. Unlike the north-Indian traders who were invited to 'start' Alleppey in the eighteenth century, the British entrepreneurs who came during the nineteenth century never became real residents. They came and went. Moreover, they normally came alone without bringing wives and offspring. In this respect too there was a considerable difference with many other towns on the subcontinent, where the 'civil lines', 'cantonments', 'railway lines', etc. were, since the second half of the nineteenth century, increasingly inhabited by British couples. The British Alleppeyans in the census year of 1901 who numbered forty persons out of a total population of about 25,000 included only three women. These British were by a vast majority single men, and young adventurists rather than long-term residents. They may well have been less concerned with public hygiene, as they came to Alleppey to make money and then left. Though their Indian colleagues and the mass of labourer stayed on, their voices were less or not yet at all heard in the official records of the late 1800s and early 1900s on which most data in this part of this chapter are based.

Altogether, it seems likely that the position of British citizens of Alleppey, living under spacious conditions near the beach and holding the view that soil and water could control hygienic problems, did not press for improvements of sanitation and other dimensions of public health. And if they would have pressed, the Commercial Agent, their compatriot, could have solved their problems. It was not before the 1890s that some form of institutionalized management of urban problems was deemed necessary, due to increasing pressure on land as the result of both the gradually growing population and the expanding trade, transport, and manufacture.

The late start of local urban government was certainly made good in an institutional sense. Around 1920 fully elected councils were inaugurated in Alleppey and elsewhere. The institutionalization of urban local government through the TIC in Alleppey meant also a de jure separation of 'port' and 'town', and a gradual separation of the specific interests.

Before 1894 the 'town' was just a part of the 'port', but from that year onwards responsibilities and tasks were separated, even though the Commercial Agent was for some time in charge of both institutions.

A NOTE ON THE MUNICIPAL COUNCIL

The main aims of the new fully elected municipal council were more or less the same as those of its predecessor: concern with and improvement of public health in the town. In 1937, for example a plague outbreak in Market Ward was fought with might and means under the direction of the council. The ward was compulsory evacuated: 278 huts and houses were burnt down, rats were destroyed, and within a week no less than 44,532 inhabitants were vaccinated (out of a total population of about 50,000). Though twenty-six deaths were counted, the plague attack was 'under control' in a fortnight (TAT 1935-6: 193). This epidemic also shows the extent of the separation of 'town' and 'port'. At the outbreak of the epidemic, which would have brought much of the economic activities of the port and the town to a standstill, a 'Special Plague Officer' was appointed by the Commercial Agent, next to the municipal organization, 'in order to prevent infection to the port and to maintain trade without interruption.' (TAR 1935-6: 173). On an earlier occasion, the municipal councillors were informed about diseases and health. The report of the state mentions that: 'The dissemination of knowledge in regard to the causes of ordinary diseases and their cure by means of magic lantern lecture was also attended by them' (TAR 1927-8: 198).

There remained much more to be worried about, notably regarding public health. Drinking water remained of a very poor quality in Alleppey, until about 1937 when a few underground water wells were tapped. Till that year impure local water was drunk by many, while the happy few bought fresh drinking water carried by *vellam* from Kottayam, 20 km away. However, in the 1960s, it was mentioned in a

Town Planning Report by the Government of Kerala, that only 34 per cent of all households in Alleppey had access to—what is called—'protected water supply' (Government of Kerala, 1966: 69). Similarly, sewerage systems left much to be desired. The same report states on page 53, that 65 per cent of all households in Alleppey used, what is called 'Open land' for defecation, while 11.5 per cent had access to sceptic tanks, 15 per cent to conservancy arrangements (private buckets, etc.) and 7.5 per cent to 'bore holes'. The 'open land' option led to severe pollution by faeces-born carriers of diseases dysentery, hookworm, given the sandy compound soils of most huts, and the unplastered lanes on which many hut-dwellers walked.

Certainly, canals were more or less continuously deepened and cleaned, and encroachments more or less continuously removed, according to the annual reports. But the municipality seems rather powerless to arrest developments which were at variance with its aim of acquiring a clean and tidy town.

NOTES

1. *Peishkar* was the highest magistrate in one of the three administrative divisions of Travancore. *Tahsildar* were in-charge of a *taluk*, a sub-division of a division.
2. I shall not elaborate here on the emergence of modern local government in India. It has been extensively researched. For a detailed introduction, see Schenk, 2020: 44-55.
3. This peculiar position of Alleppey will be discussed in the next section.
4. It would take some 40 years more before a piped drinking water system was introduced.

PART THREE
REACTIONS TO CHANGE

CHAPTER 8

Reactions to Change: Local Voices

> Now I asked Janardhan to tell me exactly what was the trouble in Alleppey. . . . He replied in one word: 'Labour'. (Peruman, 1939: 54)

> The descent was precipitous owing to a conspiracy of circumstances. (Parthasaraty, 1967)

LOCAL VOICES

In the preceding chapters the focus of attention has been on the changes which had taken place from the moment when the small village Alappuzha was transformed into a trading and industrial centre in Travancore and later Kerala: Alleppey. These changes have been discussed with the certain distance of an outsider, and relatively easy allowing for pros and cons. In this chapter I seek attention for those who had been more directly involved in such changes as citizens of the place where it all happened. I have recorded the local reactions to change during a period when especially the economic lifelines of the town corroded. Hence, outspoken reactions were to be expected, and under the conditions of economic downfall, many local opinions about 'what went wrong', were likely to be recorded. Frustration, disappointment, anger from those residents who had something to loose: influence, power, profits, could be expected then, as well as prophecies and just hopes of a better future. Or just observations could be made, from those who were not directly affected by such changes but saw it all happen and tried to understand it. Some opinions have been written down, while more are just spoken—in private or in public. Most opinions have merely been expressed; others have led to a wide range of actions as shall be seen in this chapter. Some seem dogmatic: 'The downfall of Alleppey is a historical necessity', said a civil servant, while others seem rather dramatic: 'Alleppey is the Waterloo of industrialists', in the words of an aged journalist.

Reactions to changes in Alleppey have been dealt with here in two chapters. In the next chapter (Chapter 9) the views on change by the formerly mighty industrial and trading elite of Alleppey, organized in the Travancore Chamber of Commerce, are brought to the fore and analysed. These views are taken from their annual reports, and notably from the annual speeches of their chairmen. The present Chapter 8 is less homogeneous. The following analyses of reaction and the perceptions preceding these, were partly based on open-ended interviews and discussions with a limited number of mainly elder inhabitants from a wide range of (former) walks of life.[1] I moreover gathered printed sources: papers presented at local conferences, pamphlets prepared for occasional use, 'letters to the editor' of local journals, etc., to augment the oral information. Many more documents must certainly exist, but I did not come across them.[2] For this reason the analyses in this chapter are of a limited meaning, and I cannot claim to have used a representative set of printed (and oral) voices and statements on events in Alleppey. I feel, however that I have covered the main sentiments and the main reactions. They form the building bricks of a 'history from below'.

By and large, the period covered by these sources was limited to some forty years, from the late 1930s onwards till the late 1970s. From a first assessment of the contents of the collected information, it was found that the mentioned reasons for Alleppey's downfall could rather easily be categorized under a limited number of main headings:

(a) the development of Cochin, the infrastructural facilities directed towards that town and the lack of similar facilities to the benefit of Alleppey;

(b) the tense labour relations and the role of politicians and the executive powers in that matter;
(c) the merger of Travancore and India;
(d) Alleppey's one-sided industrialization, notably in coir industries; and
(e) the rivalries between British and Indian entrepreneurs and the British departure from the coir business.

Notably 'Cochin', infrastructure and labour relations have come to the fore in the oral and written sources and will get most of the attention in this chapter too.

PERCEPTIONS OF CHANGE FOR BETTER AND FOR THE WORSE: INFRASTRUCTURE

Alleppey's growth and prosperity was related in earlier chapters to infrastructural facilities in combination with technological levels of transportation of the past. Its downfall to new technologies and new means of transport. It will be seen whether local opinions support this reasoning.

There is a clear awareness, expressed in several ways, that Alleppey owed a substantial part of its past prosperity to its specific location. Pilla, a local politician and campaigner for the coastal railway between Cochin and Alleppey, wrote in a paper, presented at the 'Seminar on development of Alleppey town', in 1971 and sponsored by the 'Junior Chamber of Alleppey':

> The most important geographic advantage of Alleppey was its accessibility. As water was the main media of bulk transport at that time, Alleppey provided the maximum accessibility at minimum costs.

His statement can often be heard and read. The threats to this (weak) economic base have been spelled out just as often. Two main arguments to substantiate the threats can be identified here: the development of roads and railroads elsewhere in the state, and the lack of similar developments directed toward the town: there were waterways plenty but roads and railroads? There was in Alleppey a certain understanding about the lack of east-west running roads to and from the town which nevertheless was used as co-explanatory for Alleppey's decay. Often, and with some irony, the story could be heard of several contractors who had gone bankrupt while they never managed to construct proper foundations to some bridges on these east-west roads, and who time and again lost the battle between a tight tender system and 'unfathomable' subsoils of the backwaters.

Contrary to the understanding about the failures to realize an east-west road to and from Alleppey, a major shock was felt by many entrepreneurs when the Government of India decided in 1954 to have a railway constructed heading south from Cochin, but running east of the backwaters, far from Alleppey. It seems that it was taken for granted in Alleppey that such a railway would pass via Alleppey. According to a railway protagonist: 'South Indian Railways wanted a line Cochin–Alleppey–Quilon, but when the British left, the whole organization collapsed'.

The discussion on the exact course of the line was focused on a perceived lack of pressure from 'Alleppey', which gave, according to local analyses, competing entrepreneurs on the other side of the backwaters in and around Kottayam, some margin to promote a favourable course to them to transport their export produce (spices, rubber, etc.) to Cochin. It might accordingly well be in these analyses, that issues of party politics played a role in the decision on the site for the railway track, and a few references pointing in that direction can be found. The Kottayam entrepreneurs and the influential local paper, the *Malayalam Manorama*, clearly represented Syrian Christian interests, which were major pillars in the region of the Congress party. However, the emerging left-wing political dominance in Travancore-Cochin originated for a great deal in Alleppey and its coastal surroundings. Notably these left-wing parties were very critical to say the least of the New Delhi-based Congress politicians who decided about the railway.

The Cochin–Kottayam–Quilon railway figures frequently in expressions of frustration, and the non-existent railway line between Alleppey and Cochin was a bitter experience for many, judging from the comments on it.

A Coastal Railway: Frustrations and Expectations

Unlike some resignation about the superiority of the port of Cochin compared to Alleppey's roadsteads, the attempts to acquire after all the 'coastal railway' was seen as a realistic goal by local interest groups. Why was it considered as important? Two elements play a role when answering this question: hurt pride and perceived economic benefits. It was said that Alleppey was considerably shocked that the railway from Cochin to the south bypassed Alleppey. Thus, from the 1950s onwards attempts were made to have the coastal railway constructed in addition to the line via Kottayam. However, it was only during the 1970s that it became a popular issue. As said, hurt pride was a first element: 'It is a shame that an industrial centre as Alleppey is not served by a railway.' And it was pointed out to a railway minister in the central government that:

> Crores of Rs. worth of foreign exchange earned through the products of this region . . . have been diverted for the development of other parts of India. . . . We are very unhappy with this discrimination. . . . (Pilla, 1966; a crore equals ten million)

Most arguments in favour of a coastal railway line were strictly economic: the line had been considered as a prerequisite and as a draught horse for economic development. The main arguments were (and most sound familiar):

- The railway is supposed to boost the economy of Alleppey by providing a better and quicker outlet for its products to the port of Cochin and to other areas in India.
- It is supposed to tap regional resources hitherto insufficiently tapped. Marine products are occasionally mentioned in this respect, as well as silica.
- The railway would bring industries to the densely populated but under-employed region between Cochin and Alleppey,

thus adding to industrial development and the generation of employment.

- In a direct way it will bring employment for no less than 2,000 people, according to J.S. Nair, President of the All Kerala Railway Users Association in a speech held in Alleppey in 1979 (Munnani, 15 April 1979).
- The railway will promote tourism ('seeing the backwaters, the paddy fields').

This list of familiar and new arguments, and compiled from several sources, is long enough. It has served as a backing for a series of actions to achieve the ultimate goal. These actions started around 1966 when K.L. Omana Pilla started 'The Alleppey-Cochin Coastal Development Council' and prepared a petition in his capacity as chairman of this council, to the central railway minister. The contents of the petition were clear; the minister was to sanction the railway 'this year itself'. From that year onwards Pilla campaigned in several elections as an independent candidate (in vain) mainly on the issue of the coastal railway. In 1970 Pilla petitioned again for sanctioning of 'the early construction' of the line. Afterwards the action broadened and was taken over by established interest groups. It figured in papers at the above-mentioned symposium in 1971, while organizations like the Travancore Chamber of Commerce (see Chapter 9) and the semi-official 'Alleppey Development Council', headed by the municipal chairman, took it up as a prime issue. Several petitions to several central railway ministers, prime ministers and members of the Planning Commission were written. On several occasions the desirability of the railway connection with Cochin was brought to the fore. The state government played a part by granting the surveying and the sleepers free of charge to the railway authorities . . . if and when.

Then, in 1979, the expected sanction was given. The daily *Indian Express* called it 'A gesture to Kerala' in a leading article, and a help 'to convince the people of Kerala that the era of neglect is over' (22 February 1979). More happened to commemorate this 'gesture':

The central railway minister came on April 15 to Alleppey to inaugurate the works. On this occasion the municipal chairman spoke in flowing terms of the history of the actions to get the railway to Alleppey: 'The railway is the slogan of the people. It will make revolutionary change in the coastal area' (*Munnani*, April 15). He honoured the many interest groups which had been dealing with the battle for it. He recalled a.o. how, in 1978, the local Development Council sent a delegation to Delhi: On 17 November 1978, the civilians of Cochin, Shertallai and Alleppey wished them success. This incident awakened spiritual feelings in the Malayali people who have settled in Madras and Pondicherry. They also came to the airport of Madras for wishing all success. The President of the All Kerala Railway Users Association spoke in similar wording, while the Travancore Chamber of Commerce gave out a press notice in which it was suggested that secret-diplomacy by its members in New Delhi had been instrumental for the positive decision (*Munnani*, April 15).

There was one largely forgotten railway champion: the originator of the action Omana Pilla. He was only honoured in a letter to the editor in the *Indian Express* of 28 February.[3]

The episode of concerted action by interest groups in Alleppey shows that action aimed at infrastructural issues (or rather: reaction originating from felt infrastructural neglects) could be taken up and brought to a success. Such action tends however to simplify local conditions. The belief that industries will now settle in the coastal belt and that employment is on its way, is rather premature and does not allow for considerations regarding other societal processes and conditions in and around Alleppey. For that reason, it seems that the most important dimension of the coastal railway issue has been that of a scapegoat and a diversionary manoeuvre hiding local problems. It is significant in this sense that the railway issue was taken up mainly by merchants, employers, etc., while trade unions did not participate prominently. The lack of a railroad served as a politically harmless rallying issue in Alleppey, whereby outsiders could safely be blamed for local social problems. Was therefore the lack of a railway a blessing in disguise? Later in this chapter will this issue be discussed in a different context.

The Port of Cochin

Closely related to the lack of roads and railroads to and from Alleppey and the existence of such means of transportation elsewhere is the development of Cochin's port and its effects on a wide region. As has been seen in earlier chapters, the construction of this port was mainly undertaken during the 1920s and 1930s: thus, it was after the Second World War that its full effects began to be felt, including the decline of the port of Alleppey. Varghese observed at the above mentioned Seminar on Development of Alleppey town in 1971: 'Cochin Port which developed as one of the major ports of the country, has absorbed part of the trade of Alleppey'. This sentence seems to be an understatement in view of the available trade statistics which show an almost complete collapse of the export trade in Alleppey by the year 1970 (see Appendix, Table 3). Other spokesmen, among whom a retired manager of one of the former leading coir manufacturing companies, were much more outspoken on the issue of 'Cochin': 'Cochin took the trade from Alleppey port, mainly as it is a well-equipped all-weather port'. Yet resignation dominated about the downfall of the port and the success of the one in Cochin. It was realized and accepted by the spokesmen with whom I discussed the port, that its success led subsequently to an axis of modern industrial development to the north-east of Cochin and created labour opportunities and additional income in the Cochin region. 'Alleppey could not compete with Cochin', can be taken as an adequate summary: the tide cannot be turned, and voices expressing the hope of such a turn were seldom heard, if at all.

PERCEPTIONS OF CHANGING LABOUR RELATIONS: WHO IS TO BLOW, WHOM IS TO BE BLOWN?

> A sweeper in the Darragh Smail Company gave a blow with his broom to his boss. [Anonymous].

In Chapter 4 the rising power of labour unions from the 1920s onwards has been mentioned. It was also seen in that chapter that the state of Travancore and entrepreneurs joined hands to control threats to the status quo of a capitalist colonial local economy. Moreover, labour relations up to the late 1930s were largely seen as just 'friendly' by those who were in command of the large and small companies in the town. A retired manager of the Alleppey factory of the Swiss firm Volkart Brothers explicitly referred to a peaceful relationship between employer and employee. However, this picture changed rapidly since the late 1930s, as measured by the strong wording in which 'labour' and related aspects such as labour unrest or exploitation of labour has been talked about by almost all respondents, including 'non-workers', and as assessed in the late 1970s.

'The main problem of Alleppey is the problem of Labour Unions', said an aged local historian, repeating what he wrote in the local daily *Munnani*:

> The relation between the merchants and labour began to lose, they demanded more and more. No sincerity in the work led the way to decline but it helped the development of the party (the Communist Party of India, HS) and labour unions. When the leaders (of trade unions, HS) and political parties developed in strength, if they got a chance, they began to give blows to the merchant and business men. It is very sad to note that these kinds of atrocities were developed from the soil of Alleppey. (Koya, 1976).

An elderly journalist put it in this way: 'All went down 100 per cent because of communist (labour unions, HS) politics', while a highly ranking Roman Catholic priest scorns at: '. . . unlimited bargaining for wages', leading to an '. . . objective lesson of what communism can do in ruining an industrial centre'.

The 'communists' and the members of trade unions held other views. They pointed at oppression, wage cuts, 'slavery', hunger:

> At that time the oil-mill labourers were not given any freedom. They lived in poor conditions. Tapioca and fish were given to labourers at lunch and suppertime. . . . The labourers got work four days a week. If the supervisor got toddy from the labourers, he would give for seven days a week. . . . There were thousands of workers in the field of spice industry, most of them were women. The contractors harassed the women and made waysides incidentally, and: The labourers were beaten by the contractor if they made mistakes in their work.

The start and building up of any organization of labourers must have been a tremendous task in the social climate of Alleppey during, say, the 1930s. However, it began, keeping a low profile at first, but gradually developing into a force to be reckoned with: a real force about demands for better wages and fringe benefits, even regarding inhuman treatment and the desire to become 'respected' and not being beaten at will. Moreover, labour unions started to be seen as a threat to the existing order. The fear that Travancore might turn into a revolutionary bastion was apparently there among eye-witnesses of the late 1930s and the 1940s.

'Trade union leaders misused the literacy of workers to mislead them', a spokesman said, while several others used more or less identical words: 'workers could read but not evaluate properly.' And thus, left-wing ideas were brought into the heads of thousands of labourers, as is even now recalled with horror by opponents of a growing consciousness among the rank and file of the Alleppey labour force. Innocent heads, they were, writes Koya: 'The people who worked in the European companies and warehouses were completely satisfied with their income' (1976), while Prasad nuanced considerably: 'The bulk of our working people were content in the old days with sub-human standards of living, but today we think of a welfare state, quite rightly, since becoming free' (1971).

In this way a picture was formed and framed: innocent and happy workers were indoctrinated by unscrupulous trade union leaders and 'communists'. A major perception of change among those who had something to lose and of those who had something to gain seems to be in the apprehension of the process of emancipation of Alleppey's labour force. Contours of this process have been given in an earlier chapter, in terms of change in the economic structure of society: slaves and Ezhavas became labourers, capitalist entrepreneurs entered the local society. Social aspects of change led to emotions among those who had something to lose. For example, managers, contractors and supervisors dealt blows to workers as they saw that as an appropriate way of establishing societal or just simply work floor hierarchies. In the 1960s, however: 'A sweeper in the Darragh Smail Company gave a blow with his broom to his boss'. This single fact is recorded and told by some as proof of the deterioration of all that was accepted among the elites in the former days: who is to blow, whom to be blown. A foundation of society shattered.

Some spokesmen and local authors give a less simple analysis of the labour dimension in Alleppey's downfall. There is among them a feeling that labourers were worse off in the 1930s than now; that they were exploited, though some justification is always given (labourers having few desires, less than now), as a few quotations above show. Among the more sophisticated analyses of 'what went wrong' in Alleppey, mention is made of undercutting by Indian entrepreneurs since the 1930s. It is alleged that Indian coir manufacturers and shippers tried to get a share in the market by selling at lower prices, and probably by paying lower wages. These firms spoiled the market, it was said, also in terms of inferior products sent abroad, giving Indian mats and matting a bad name and thus helping to kill the industry in the long run. Similarly, among those more sophisticated analyses, inter-trade union rivalries have often been mentioned.

Thus, a share of 'labour unrest' has been attributed to entrepreneurial cut-throat competition to the detriment of labour and the quality of the produce. The retired managers whom I met spoke in such a way. Moreover, the Factory Act, gradually implemented after the Second World War, replaced contractors, and the coir companies had to employ their labourers directly. And entrepreneurs had to pay the statutory wages due to trade union power. The labour unions concentrated their efforts to get the laws implemented on foreign firms, as these could be marked as the most outspoken exponents of capitalism and imperialism. 'Destroy Capitalism' became one of the labour slogans since late 1930s (Jeffrey, 1984). A spokesman—a retired clerk of a British coir company—commented dryly on the foreign reactions: 'The European firms quietly packed and left', while another, a Roman-Catholic priest, added: 'They took with them the most valuable machinery'.

Related to 'irresponsible behaviour' of the trade union leaders, the competition among several trade unions working in the same industry has been seen as a cause for the decline of industrial and other economic activities in Alleppey. The picture of leaders of competing unions outbidding each other is given: in order to attract members, to gain in popularity and power, but causing 'on many occasions ruin of the trade itself' (Narayan Nair, 1971). Inter-trade union competition is rather common in India, but it does not fit well with the alleged 'communist indoctrination' of workers. Rather it implies a much more pragmatic functioning of unions from the perspective of the workers: the delivery of the fruits counted. Moreover, it must be remarked here that employers themselves initiated rivalling unions—even in the 1930s—in the hope to split up and divide workers. This will be discussed in the next section where the question is posed how 'vested interests' reacted on their loss of power, prestige and profits.

DIVIDE, ACCOMMODATE, BUT SURVIVE AND RULE: REACTIONS TO CHANGING AND CHANGED LABOUR RELATIONS

Reactions to a changing (and often changed) social structure and the changing positions of labourers in it were manifold. A few major reactions will be dealt with here. Direct confrontations on the work floor were involved, were conscious workers demanded higher wages or a more human treatment, and when only a very cold shoulder was given. Pramani recalls an example of such a confrontation among fishermen immediately before and leading to the 'Punnapra-Vayalar uprising', important for the history of the Indian trade union movement,[4] in 1946:

> Before this struggle the condition of the fishermen in Kerala was that of slaves. In Vadakkal there was a big landowner, Aplon Aroj. . . . He had 5 boats and under him 80 fishermen were working. His business was buying large quantities of fish from those boats at low prices. The fishermen . . . had no right to discuss the price. . . . How hard they worked, there was no question of getting more money, so that most of them led a life in terrible poverty.[5]
>
> In this situation, Michael, who was a fisherman, came forward as a leader. He organized all the fishermen . . . in order to save the lives of the fishermen from slavery. . . . Accordingly . . . they organized their own union and its leaders questioned Aroj about the price of fish. But that was an unexpected voice for Aplon, because nobody questioned him before. Within seconds the three leaders were tied on three coconut trees by rowdies of Aroj, who beated [*sic*] up the leaders mercilessly. Then he called the police and they also beated [*sic*] and treated them cruelly. . . . (Pramani, 1971)

Beating, harsh treatment, intimidation, were rather 'normal' acts from the side of entrepreneurs, as was seen earlier, and was recalled by other labour leaders. However, growing unity among workers (especially the coir worker who organized themselves at an early stage) made employers realize that more effective ways of control over labourers had to be found. The basic counterstrategy was for some time to divide labourers into conflicting camps. For this purpose, a Catholic Labour Union was formed, as early as 1936, under the umbrella of the Roman Catholic Church. A member of another trade union remembers: 'The members who attended (the first meeting, HS), were priests and supporters of Christianity'. Besides, coir factory owners attended its inauguration and promoted its growth. An informant, however, proudly recalled that the then existing unions opposed the idea of a communal union, and apparently the Catholic union could not become a viable proposition to out-manoeuvre others. Shortly after Second World War a similar attempt was made to start a Catholic union under the auspices of the Bishop of Alleppey. The idea was to start an 'independent trade union' (the ITU) to counter the then mighty conglomerate of unions under the umbrella of the Communist Party of India (CPI) related All India Trade Union Congress (AITUC). This independent union failed again, due, as it was said, to misappropriation of the union funds by a leader, and in the early 1950s a third attempt was made. At that time, the political spectrum was broadened, by a merger of Catholic aspirations and attempts of the Congress party and its affiliated Indian National Trade Union Congress (INTUC) to get a foothold in Alleppey. This attempt succeeded more or less and hitherto the union-scene was characterized by two major unions. After the split in the CPI in 1964, the Centre of Indian Trade Unions (CITU) was formed, related to the new Communist Party of India (Marxist): CPI(M). So, after all, employers got what they wanted originally: competing unions. However, at that time the economic conditions, under which trade unions were active had changed so much that organized labour realized that it had to cooperate rather than to compete. Now and then, the unions joined hands and divided their interests, geographically within the town, or otherwise. In that way they were able to defend their meagre interests for their members (see Schenk-Sandbergen, 1988),[6] and actually oppose the former divide-and-rule strategy of entrepreneurs.

Other forms of reactions till the late 1940s included the calling in of police assistance as was shown above. Till that time the police did come, but police help and a more or less unconditional state support for entrepreneurs dwindled with the merger of Travancore with India in 1949 and a resulting new power structure at state level. In this respect an irreversible process of change had taken place. In a similar way provided new labour acts for such an irreversible process, as well the Industrial Tribunals, set up in 1947 to solve labour disputes, in spite of entrepreneurial protests. It is not the purpose of this chapter to give a more exhaustive list of such developments. The mentioned examples serve as signals of a changing structure of labour relations, against which those who were on the losing side protested and tried to act.

Sadly enough, the most powerful reaction proved to be the retreat from Alleppey by those entrepreneurs who could afford to retreat. But retreat cannot simply be considered as a defeat. In preceding chapters, the decline of the demand for coir products (and on a much smaller scale also that of coconut oil) has been mentioned as a major cause of the 'crisis in the coir industry' as it has been called. Alleppey was hit hard by this crisis: it added to its technological and infrastructural outdatedness. These factors should be seen in combination with the changing labour relations: all together they can explain this retreat. During the years of prosperity in the coir industry margins were always found to meet labour demands to a small extent. When profits faded away, each negative change could make a company or a small entrepreneur decide to stop, or to stop in Alleppey.

Some companies—some foreign companies—went 'home', partly taking up manufacturing of finished coir products to Britain or elsewhere, while buying raw material through their agents at Alleppey. Or they stayed on a minimal basis as a shipper of coir products made for them by order in household scale manufacturing units. Other companies left for Cochin to ensure better transport facilities, while others again found a 'quieter' industrial climate in other Indian states, where labour legislation was enforced less. Retreat without defeat was present as a major counter strategy of vested interests. The retreat served to safeguard gains.

Finally, those who stayed, 'went underground' and made deals with the seeming victors. As was heard from several sides and admitted occasionally in the open, accounts were falsified to subvert sales taxes and company taxes or factory act regulations. Arrangements were made with political parties and trade unions to ensure a smooth functioning of a factory without strikes; labourers were occasionally told by employers not to join a trade union and were rewarded for it, etc. The stayers on—and most of the entrepreneurs had to stay—had to accommodate to changing conditions and they did so on the best possible terms. The seeming victors, however, found a mare's nest. Trade unions could to some degree control the local economy, since the 1960s, but the more they reached this stage, the less was there to control. Jobs disappeared when they were better rewarded, fringe benefits dissolved as *fata morganas*. 'Respectability' was acquired, or enforced, but the chances to live a respectable life diminished. In this way, and to this extent, entrepreneurial reactions to change proved effective: they were effective in the sense that their counter actions left the recipients of change without the means to consume their gains. Unlike the seemingly concerted action to get a railway line to Alleppey, the reactions discussed in this section under the banner 'Divide, accommodate, but survive and rule' left Alleppey in ruins, labour being allowed to raise red flags on the debris, while at the same time somewhat comfortable shelters underneath it were available to those who formally lost the battle.

HOPES AND DREAMS

Expectations for a better future had been expressed. Some of these dreams seem well founded. The railway will come, was the assurance in 1979, and no doubt, it would have effected the employment situation in the region and on the structure of the local economy. But there was in the late 1970s also a good deal of wishful thinking about the magic of a railway. The boundary line between relatively well-founded expectations and less well-founded hopes is difficult to draw.

Hopes and dreams of many kinds were present in Alleppey. Alleppey might develop as a tourist centre, as had already been said as a rationale for the railway line. Several spokesmen pictured Vembanad Lake and the many waterways of the backwaters full of houseboats, water-skiers and other sporters, flanked by anglers and picknickers.[7] Others visualize an 'aerodrome' and see a big jump into modern means of transport bringing Alleppey back on the world transportation map. It is here that hopes get mixed up with dreams.[8] Hopes are present about new industries, and of a broader and more modern industrial base in a development region between Cochin and Alleppey. Pilla expressed the hope that Alleppey could get a good deal of the industrial overflow of congested Cochin, if there were roads and a railway (1971), while Prasad wrote in 1971:

> . . . if there is an industrial belt between Cochin and Alwaye (north-east of Cochin, HS), which impediments are there for an industrial belt to develop Cochin and Alleppey? . . . The inland water transport is even now better developed between Cochin–Alleppey than between Cochin–Alwaye.

Such hopes elaborate on roads, a railway and an airport, but others (also) on 'labour'. It is at this point that changes and their reactions seem to melt together, and a picture emerges of a new-Alleppey, equipped with modern infrastructural facilities, a more modern industry and more 'balanced' labour relations. Do thesis and a subsequent antithesis finally produce an all-encompassing synthesis? I shall examine this hope a little bit. At the above-mentioned Seminar on the development of Alleppey, even middle-class participants expressed some sympathy with labour: 'There is no escape from cooperation between labourer and capital if we are to live and become a prosperous people' remarked Prasad in his contribution to the Seminar (in 1971), and he added:

> I believe enlightened labour and capital leadership in Alleppey have realized this, but we have yet to work out schemes practically, highlighting labour-capital cooperation.

In 1979 more voices were heard regarding some sort of reconciliation with 'labour' or of stabilization of labour relations. 'Factory workers are quiet now. They have learned that violence is not good', said an informant. Labourers and trade union leaders expressed themselves in a similar way, though of course turning the above statement around: 'Capitalists have learned a lot. We get better treatment now. They have to listen to us.'

Non-working class observers of the local society may also point out a rift between labourers and their leaders, in trade unions and in politics: 'Labourers have become more independent because of frustrating experiences of last 25 years.' It was said and also others bring this up—or is this wishful thinking? One step further is taken by 'embracing' labour: 'The Alleppey workers are very good workers', and aged man said, and 'Nowhere are there so many skilled workers with natural gift', a pepper merchant remarked.

Taking the comments together, a future image of hope expressed by local inhabitants gradually appears. Enlightened cooperation between labour and capital should and will come (or is already there latently). But one has to remain sceptical as well about Alleppey's future. A 'new' Alleppey will have few of the advantages of the old in the eyes of prospective entrepreneurs. Its former low-cost infrastructure is hardly relevant; its subservient labour force is of the past. But what then will attract entrepreneurs to the town? The abundant size of its labour force is hardly exceptional in India. Are there new, yet unexplored, dimensions of such a 'new' Alleppey? Is 'tourism' an unexplored hope or dream? I shall come to that in the Epilogue.

NOTES

1. I had semi-structured discussions and interviews with twenty people, between February and June 1979 and in December 1981. Many of them I met several times. The following categorization indicates their personal and social backgrounds: Two clerks of coir companies (both retired); three civil servants (one retired); two merchants; three leaders of trade unions; one shopkeeper; four professionals

(lawyer, two journalists—one retired, clergy); three having various occupations.

2. A full list of consulted sources of this kind is given in a separate section of the list of references (sources published in Alleppey).
3. The letter, by Kalathil, should be quoted here in full. 'Sir, Mr. K.L. Omana Pillai of Alleppey deserves the warmest congratulations from the people of Kerala, especially those of Alleppey, for incessant efforts to get the coastal railway line sanctioned by the Centre. Thrice he contested the elections on this particular issue with the sole intention of educating the people about the necessity of a railway line linking Alleppey and Cochin. Once his election symbol itself was the train. His assertion that the past glory of Alleppey—once known as the Venice of the East and the most important commercial centre of Travancore—could be regained only if this railway line came to its rescue, was in those election times pooh-poohed by all political parties who now claim credit for getting it. Some spoke of him in those days as an eccentric and others mocked him by calling him "coastal railway", "electric train", etc.' It is true that all parties tried and worked for the coastal railway later, but we should all remember with gratitude the fact that it was Mr. Pillai who took the initiative in this matter. The authorities should have studied his request to introduce electric trains instead of ordinary trains on this line in view of the fact we have enough and more of electric power. (Pilla used to spell his name without an ending 'i', though others did not always do so, HS).
4. See for more details on this well-known uprising, which originated in two villages near Alleppey, a.o. Kusuman, 1977; Ouwerkerk, 1994; Heller, 1999.
5. Kusuman adds in a sarcastic manner some more details of the earnings of the fishermen and other involved parties. The owners of the boats took half of the earnings, and the other half was for the crew: 'Thus the returns, when it came to a man's share were all but encouraging. Then came the share of God (the fisherman in the region were Latin Catholics, HS), who was so rapacious as the owner in soliciting his share. So too was the share claimed on behalf of the deceased elders of the owner.' (1977: 52)
6. Schenk-Sandbergen wrote about this: 'The very bad economic situation forced the trade-union(s) to become so to say "employers"

for their members. To realize this . . . they fought a real life-and-death struggle to "conquer" areas of the town to monopolize coolie work there for their own members. . . . It can be stated that in 1979 along the two main canals of Alleppey . . . all central points, and especially bridges are occupied by either INTUC or AITUC or CITU'. (1988: 65)

7. I shall come back to the dream of Alleppey as a water-tourist centre in the final Epilogue.
8. Again, Cochin hijacked this dream. Cochin has an airport, with national and international scheduled flights.

CHAPTER 9

Reactions to Change: Voices from a Trading Elite in Alleppey

THE TRAVANCORE CHAMBER OF COMMERCE

The Travancore Chamber of Commerce (TCC), an organization of elite merchants and industrialists in and around Alleppey is analysed regarding its views on what happened and still happens in the local society, in Kerala, in India, and finally in 'the world' during a period of about thirty years from the independence of India onwards.

The TCC was established in 1928. Before 1947, the Chamber was primarily an organization of export-oriented entrepreneurs in Travancore. Though as such its base was larger than that of Alleppey proper, it was only natural that the TCC settled in this town. Within Travancore no other urban place could challenge Alleppey in terms of export trade, as was seen in previous chapters. Many of the merchants in the TCC formed chains in trade relations between Travancore and Britain (and to some extent, other European and Anglo-Saxon countries). A few were engaged in one single chain, like trade; others were active in more ways: they could own plantations, have interests in shipping companies, run coir factories, etc. Some merchants specialized in one specific product, such as spices (hill produce): other traded in many items, both exporting and importing all kind of articles. Many merchants extracted raw materials from Travancore for processing and consumption abroad; others developed into industrialists, making finished products for the world at large (coir!) and grew beyond a more typical role in a colonial process of extraction.

The firm of Peirce, Leslie & Co., Ltd, for example, which was on the Malabar Coast since 1862 with several establishments (such as a coir factory in Alleppey), was active in many commercial and industrial fields. The list of its trade in tropical products includes the following items:

> Aloe fibre, Aloe yarn, Annatto seeds, Bees wax, Bombay mace, Bone grist, Canes, Capsicums, Cardamoms, Cashew kernels, Cashew shell liquid, Chaulmoogra oil, Cinchona bark, Coconut oil, Coculus Indicus, Coffee, Coir fibre, Coir mats, Coir matting, Coir ropes, Coir yarn, Copra, Ebony, Fish guano, Fish oil, Ginger groundnuts, Gum damar, Jute matting, Laurelwood, Lemongrass oil, Manioc meal, Maroti oil, Myrobalans, Nux vomica, Palm nuts, Palmyra fibre, Pepper, Poona, Rosewood, Rubber, Sandalwood, Sandalwood oil, Sapan wood, Soap nuts, Tak, Turmeric, Vanilla. (Langley, n.d.: 46)

Besides this, the company held shipping agencies and an insurance agency. It sold gasoline, imported Ford automobiles and many other goods from Europa. In 1968 the company came into Indian hands.

The merchants united in the TCC were predominantly foreigners:

> Englishmen, Scotsmen, representatives of an American firm, and a few Swiss. They accentuated the dominance of the British Empire over the export trade of Travancore. From 1928 till 1953 a Briton ('Britisher') was President of the TCC.[1]

Until the same year foreigners held the majority in the Committee of the Chamber. Until the mid-1950s many Britons were present at the annual meetings of the TCC, together with the Swiss representative of Volkart Brothers.[2] The Europeans were till that time mentioned first in the records of the meetings of the Chamber. It is only since the mid-1950s that Europeans and Indian were mixed on paper, but at that time the foreigners were already gradually disappearing from Alleppey.

The last Britons represented Aspinwall & Co (until 1956) and William Goodacre & Sons till the early 1960s at the TCC meetings. The last foreign representative of Darragh Smail left in 1958, the last Swiss in the late 1950s as well: an era was over.[3]

The TCC can be characterized as an organization of 'big business' in and around Alleppey. Certainly, before the Second World War, its members typically represented the large-scale companies in the town. The coir manufacturing units employed several thousands of workers, also the spice traders belonged to the major entrepreneurs in terms of employment and in terms of turnover of the trade.

A list of registered factories, as per 31 December 1964—hence in a period in which the economic importance of Alleppey was rapidly going downhill, as has been seen in Chapter 3—shows the position of the TCC. In this list 153 companies with in total 9,500 workers were presented. Of these, only twenty were united in the TCC, but these twenty companies had not less than 3,860 workers on their payroll: about 40 per cent of the enumerated workers in registered enterprises.

The TCC counted thirty two members in 1947. This number increased to fifty-eight in 1974.[4] There was a sizeable movement of incoming and outgoing companies, especially since the 1950s. From the thirty-two members in 1947, eighteen continued to be member till 1967. Of the twenty-seven new members between 1948 and 1951, only six were left in 1970. This means that membership became more short lived: many companies joined the Chamber but left after a year or after a few years. This may have to do with a changing and less stable structure of entrepreneurial activities since the 1950s. It may also indicate a decreased significance of the TCC as an export-oriented lobby of entrepreneurs. Especially this latter assumption will be raised in this chapter.

Especially since the 1960s companies which were apparently not engaged in export trade gained membership. During the 1960s a gold smith, a pharmaceutical company, a firm producing plastic articles, and a printing press joined the

TCC, to give a few examples of the new types of member-enterprises who catered to a local, a regional, but in any case, to the Indian market. This may have changed the character of he TCC and of the opinions of its members on relevant matters. Other interests were added to its former almost exclusive attention to foreign trade matters, as will also be seen further in this Chapter.

THE ANNUAL REPORTS OF THE TRAVANCORE CHAMBER OF COMMERCE AS A SOURCE OF RESEARCH

The central questions in this Chapter are how the TCC viewed the world outside the premises of the Chamber during the dramatic period of decay of economic activities since the early 1950s. And then: how did it respond to challenges to its positions brought about by the re-configuration of economic, political and social power in south-west India? Answers to these questions are mainly based on available publications of the TCC itself. The Chamber published annual reports which have been analysed for the period between 1946-7 and 1973-4 (the Chamber year runs from 1 July-30 June).

These reports consist generally of the following components:

(a) a list of members;
(b) a review of activities of the committee;
(c) financial information;
(d) report of the annual meeting, including its major element: the annual speech of the president;
(e) statistics of imports and exports, shipping, port-duties, with some comparison with other (former) Travancore ports;
(f) list of presidents and 'honorary secretaries' (the latter till 1949-50) and subsequently of vice-presidents.

For some years some elements of this list are lacking, while from 1973-4 onwards no annual reports have been published.

A printed annual speech by the president for 1978-9 finalizes the available information; other speeches during the 1970s seem to have been lost.

Most of the contents of this chapter originate in the annual speeches which can be seen as the major political statements of the TCC: 'States of the Union', so to say. It is rewarding to analyse their contents as they contain a wide range of topics and include a wide variety of points of view taken towards such topics. A view of the world is expressed in these speeches and offered to the members of the Chamber. It seems to be a world that is often centred at the headquarters of the TCC in Chamber Road, Alleppey. Moreover, it seems to be a world composed of inter-connected, concentric circles making several rings around the TCC. The outer ring is considered the most important of all. It consists of international trade, the idea of an international trade community and the role of the TCC-members therein. Through the eyes of the Chamber presidents, foreign trade exists to serve mankind and it is a pre-condition for peace and prosperity. Each hindrance to it is an evil to be banned. The second ring consists of state power and state policies—till 1949 Travancore, afterwards India; and, till 1956 also that of Travancore-Cochin and from 1956 Kerala. The TCC sees this second ring as designed to serve the international trade interests and opposes any threat to this idea. The same applies to the third ring: Alleppey and its surroundings, or rather, the conglomerate of physical, social and administrative facilities which should be present to promote trade and industry, including the mass of labourers which should be at its command. Thus, the local roads should be in a good condition (or rather those roads which have a commercial function). In this way, the TCC-statements pretend to be relevant to Alleppey in a wide sense. As it was said: 'what is good for General Motors is good for America', the TCC tended to equate the interests of its members with those of the local society, those of the nation, and those of the world. This pretention makes it relevant in this chapter to investigate the nature of the attitudes, opinions, etc. of the

TCC. Though the Chamber considers international trade of the utmost importance, 'circumstances' force its presidents to devote considerable attention in their speeches to the middle and inner rings. Often then, with some *dédain*, references were made to 'the powers that be' which interfered in the dealings of the Chamber.

The three concentric circles of attention will also form the basic structure of this chapter. The opinions of the TCC presidents in their annual speeches about each circle will be discussed in some detail. Additional information is sometimes added as seems necessary or pertinent.

VIEWS OF THE CHAMBER: WORLD TRADE

FREE TRADE

International trade is of a world wide nature and thus world politics are loosely followed by the TCC. Law and order should reign all over the world as every disruption hinders trade and transport. From this view on peace and war, several comments have been made on events abroad, with a focus on its impact on trade. As far as 'foreign countries' are involved, their import restrictions and tariffs on products from Alleppey take a central position in the attention of the Chamber, alongside the desire for political stability. 'Free trade' is the adage of the TCC, seemingly for 'scientific' reasons. 'The history of controls all the world over, according to a Reader's Digest article in 1952, has been a dismal failure, imposition for violation not withstanding', remarked president V.J. Joseph in his annual speech in 1966 (1966: 17).[5] This free trade adage is bothersome enough to the TCC members. Speculation, hoarding hazardous 'harvests' of hill produce, buyer's and seller's markets, formation of cartels, etc., may all influence the 'free market' and may lead to sizeable profits and sizeable losses in the trade. It was—in 1952—remarked: 'If fortunes were made, they were easily lost too, and losses are seldomly noticed or cared for' (1952: 15). These remarks accentuate the position of foreign trade merchants in Alleppey, or rather, their traditional position of merchant-adventurers in a free trade jungle in which the lucky ones could grow rich overnight, while many unlucky onset went bankrupt, but in which 'regulations' were rejected. This position will be illustrated in general in this section, while subsequently some special attention will be given to the pepper trade.

Soon after the trade boom immediately after Second World War, president R.H. Cass warned that 'The post war era of prosperity' was in danger, and that: '. . . most of us are probably wondering how in the current year profits are going to cover overheads'. The coming problems, according to Cass, were rooted in import restrictions to free trade, leading to his statement that: It sounds almost a paradox to couple a shortage of good with a falling profits' (1947: 13). Though the TCC members were more satisfied in the following few years, they kept on warning against political interference in trade, while in 1949 the free trade philosophy was spelled out again by Cass:

> There can be no denying the fact that every country is dependent for its very existence on the prosperity of its trade. Without that trade prosperity, no country can have either external or internal security. It is from its trade only that a country can obtain the resources to provide its required armed forces—still likely to be a necessity for some long time to come—and those social services which are required to produce internal betterment and therefore internal security. (1949, p. 11)

Three years later, president H. Smith found an opportunity to repeat this formula in the presence of an honorary guest, the chief minister of Travancore-Cochin. He asked the government to support the merchants of Alleppey who are: 'agents of production of wealth which means well being' (1952: 15).

Occasionally, Indian export restrictions (duties) were condemned too as will be seen in a later section in this chapter. But 'the other end' of the trade chain bothered the TCC more. In this respect the impending membership of Great Britain of the European Economic Community was feared in 1961, as it meant the exchange of a free trade partner for protectionist European trade policies. On the other hand, a hopeful account was given of the proceedings of a GATT-conference—how naïve this may sound afterwards:

All of us owe a deep debt of gratitude to the Hon'ble Commerce and Industry Minister Sir K.C. Reddy for his laudable and successful efforts at the recent CATT conference in Geneva where he was able to persuade the industrially advanced participating countries to reduce, or if possible, to remove completely, their import quotas and tariffs on their imports of manufactured goods from the less developed countries to which they were giving financial and economic assistance, as otherwise the value of their aid will be nullified to a great extent. We shall now wait and see how these countries react in practice to the decisions of the GATT Conference. (1961: 14)

During the 1960s, a decisive change from free trade philosophies towards current realities became manifest. In 1968-9 a request was made to 'regulate' rubber imports in order to protect the rubber planters in Kerala (1969: 19). This plea is a long way from free trade, but it was written down without any comment. It appears rather that the free trade philosophy, including its 'scientific underpinning' proved to be a profitable desire of exporters, and a less desired one of businessmen operating in the home market, like the members at the rubber-plantation. It is likely that this change of opinion can be related to the change in type of members of the Chamber since the 1960s, as was mentioned above. But, on the other hand, Britain's entry into the EEC was commented upon again in 1972, and pessimistic views on the protectionist policies of the European Community were expressed.

The topic of international trade has not been mentioned since 1972. But then international trade had been decimated as has been discussed in Chapter 3, and apparently the traders had realized this. Only 'smuggling' was discussed in those years—a plea for a 'crackdown on smugglers' was made in 1974—though one may argue that the smugglers of the 1970s were not entirely different from the merchant-adventurers within the East India Company and outside it, who, since the 1700s, had settled along the coast of Malabar and sought their commercial profits, at gun point if necessary.

THE PEPPER TRADE

> Pepper is our chief wealth (TCC, 1958: 14).

The pepper trade can be seen as a subdued free trade. The restrictions on it originate mainly from the Indian export duties and from price agreements among buyers abroad. The Indian government aimed at directing the pepper trade to hard-currency countries by a licensing system, and the export was taxed. This did not matter very much to the Chamber during the very few years after Second World War when the trade boom was enormous. The pepper exporters in Alleppey earned rupees three million in 1946-7 but rupees fifty-three million in 1949-50. The price per kg rose during those years from Rs. 2 to Rs. 11. The rise in turnover and prices was explained by the termination of Indonesian exports. Obviously the TCC members were happy. President Hann commemorated the 'unprecedent prosperity in the trade' (1950: 21). One year later however, a downfall started, and this made Hann complain again about the restrictions on free trade:

> Fiscal measures by way of duties on export of raw material offend against traditional economic canons. But traditional economic theories, however sound they may be, are another casualty of the last war. (1951: 24)

Though in the following years the claims by the Indian government to partake in the pepper-profits were accepted, it was remarked that export-duties should not be raised when the value of the exports declined. Indeed, in 1953 the trade boom was over. Both supplies and kilogram-prices declined sharply, and the pepper market turned into a buyer's market, the more so since the foreign buyers organized themselves into a cartel. It took twenty more years before the pepper-exporting countries could organize themselves into a 'pepper-OPEC', aiming at breaking the price monopoly imposed by the buyers' organizations (1972: 33). The attitude of the TCC towards the pepper trade shows the same change from acceptance of (restricted) free trade to support for state protection. Trade as free as possible was advocated during the period of boom. When the tide turned, state support was asked for—like in the early 1970s, but also in the early 1950s. A couple of years later the state was even requested to subsidize the growing and exporting of pepper in answer to similar practices in Indonesia and Brazil.

VIEWS OF THE CHAMBER: ALLEPPEY PVT. LTD. VERSUS THE REPUBLIC OF INDIA INC.

The intermediate ring around the TCC is formed by the opinions of the Chamber regarding the desired and the actual role of the national and the state governments: i.e. that of Travancore during a few years, that of Travancore-Cochin till 1956, subsequently that of Kerala, and of course that of their national Government of India. A number of sectors of contact between state(s) and Chamber come to the fore: the idea of a 'servants state', democracy, laws, taxes and development policies.

Civil Servants

The view of the TCC of the relation between state and traders can be summarized in a nutshell: we merchants bring the badly needed foreign currency for the development of India; therefore leave us in peace, do not interfere in our business, even support us in order to enable us to deliver the dollars, pounds sterling, marks and yen. Guided by this idea, the TCC welcomed the independence of India and the merger of Travancore with India. Though no direct approval can be recorded around 1947, the critical and disappointed remarks in later years indicate the positive feelings in the beginning. The 'afterthoughts' came within a few years. The Indian government tried to get a grip on trade and industry soon after its independence by way of much legislation. Several TCC presidents started subsequently to complain that the state did not allow entrepreneurs to look after the welfare of all Indians, but tried to interfere directly on their behalf at the cost of business interests. Carefully in 1950, but openly in 1952, the presidents wondered what the advantages of joining the Indian Union actually were (1950: 16; 1952: 20). Criticism, disappointment, annoyance, and protest about India's policies mark the speeches between 1950 and 1965. Before 1950 a rather hopeful perspective of the future prevailed; after 1965 the critical voices disappeared. Since the mid-1960s the criticisms became more directed toward 'harmless' matters, like the working of the telephone system. It seems that a certain resignation set in, at least a public resignation: the TCC had fought a battle and lost. However, it may well be that since then the TCC members have found it more rewarding not to utter their negative comments openly but rather to employ underground loopholes to safeguard their interests.

This change in openly expressed attitudes is of course related to the position of the TCC in Travancore before 1949. Travancore State was relatively strongly influenced by and committed to its entrepreneurial elites and its policies were strongly directed in favour of business interests. The state chose, e.g. to suppress the so-called Punnapra-Vayalar uprising in 1946 to the benefit of the merchants, without much consideration for the protesting workers. After 1947, the matter-of-factness of state policies in favour of business interests faded and the entrepreneurs had to adapt to this new social and political climate. This was most directly the case in 1957 when the Communist Party of India won the state elections and formed the first Communist government in Kerala.[6] The entrepreneurs had to find new ways of promoting their interests. Protests mark these ways between 1950 and 1965, 'silence' after 1965.

Entrepreneurs and Democracy

In 1947, the Maharaja of Travancore granted 'full responsible government to his people', i.e. he installed parliamentary democracy in Travancore, following his decision to merge his state with India (1947: 12). President Cass added that the trading community was willing to advise and support this new type of government. But in 1951, the helpful approach had already disappeared. President Cass remarked that entrepreneurial points of view were seldom heard in the legislative assembly, in which the traders 'unfortunately have no representatives' (1951: 17-8).

Nostalgia for the former corporative legislative structure was even more openly voiced in 1952, when the new democratic system was criticized: '. . . realizing that democratic elections cannot ensure direct or facultative representation in the legislature to commercial and industrial organizations' (1952: 15). The then present guest of honour, the chief minister of Travancore-Cochin, A.J. John, could not resist the temptation to ventilate his attitude towards democracy, and to counter the nostalgia for a corporate democratic structure in the Chamber. From his speech, fully included in the annual report, the following is quoted:

> You know, adult suffrage is a natural corollary of the acceptance of the maxim that sovereignty rests with the people. The rise of universal adult franchise engenders an egalitarian distribution of the right to vote and terminates professional and facultative representation in the counsels of the nation. Thus, under democracy the experts have necessarily to forego the privilege of representation as such. In spite of the above handicap, they are, and they shall always be, called upon to function in the more important role of advisors to the chosen representatives of the people. So, under the democratic set-up, the responsibilities of the industrial and business leaders are really augmented. In this way you are called away from the field of sectional advocacy to the higher sphere of expert pilotage in the problems incidental to commonweal. (1952: 27)

The TCC attitude towards 'democracy' should not be seen in isolation. It is no doubt related to the parliamentary decisions unfavourable to its interests. The trading community in Alleppey became conscious that it could no longer steer societal developments in India as it did in Travancore. That means that two distinct changes took place:

(a) 'bad' laws according to the business community replaced 'sensible' laws, and;
(b) laws were made without its direct involvement.

Moreover, the degree of implementation of many laws—such as labour legislation—was relatively high in Kerala, and this will have added to the critical view of the fruits of India's parliamentary democracy.

Labour Legislation and Taxation

The trading community had problems in adapting to new state procedures as was seen above. These problems cannot be isolated from the contents of these procedures: to some extent the rules of the game may matter, but after all it is a matter of pence. More pennies from foreign trade were gradually demanded by others: labourers, the state exchequer, and this finally determined TCC attitudes towards government policies. This becomes clear when state policies 'costing money' to entrepreneurs (minimum wages, taxes) were at stake.

Without doubt the young Indian government was active in the field of legislation. New laws replaced outdated and 'colonial' laws, and additional laws were made. As the central government was determined to perform an active part in reshaping Indian society, it is clear that some of these laws were designed to tap more and new resources.[7] The TCC vehemently and incessantly opposed state and central government in their endeavour to raise money. Basically, three lines of open defence had been put up:

(a) taxes, duties are too high;
(b) they are too much directed towards special societal categories, like entrepreneurs; and
(c) taxation measures follow one another too quickly.

A similar attitude was taken towards aspects of social legislation, embedded e.g. in the Factories Act and the minimum wages acts. The roots of this latter legislation are different, but on the premises of the TCC members they seemed to be similar to taxation: both 'cost money' to the entrepreneurs and can here be dealt with together. The three lines of defence mentioned above, manifest themselves in openly expressed protests, etc. In addition, there is a second approach: that of evasion of paying taxes and wages. This second reaction is discussed at the end of this section.

Of course, taxes are too high in the eyes of the TCC members. From 1947 to 1978 the subsequent presidents complained about the level of taxation, about high duties and about the costs of labour legislation. In 1947 President Cass complained about 'the present heavy load of taxation on industry and the individual' (1947: 20-1), while in 1978 President Walicha mentioned the very heavy 'present tax burden' (1979: 13). During in-between years similar words were spoken. Anger was mostly directed towards the sales tax and the income tax; to the Companies Act and the factory acts.[8] Such laws have a negative psychological impact on the 'business executive', complained Sulaiman Sait in 1955, as he had to devote more time to these laws than to his business (1954-5: 15). But the major point is of course that the 'executive' found them too expensive.

I will give an example of the level of the negative impact from, e.g. income tax. In 1972 the TCC discussed the so-called Wanchoo report in which a downward revision of personal income taxes was advocated. President George did not bother to deal with all these revision proposals, but confined himself to the highest tax level only, for which the report suggested a downward revision from 97.5 to 75 per cent of tax income. George complained bitterly about the Indian government that did not follow this 'worthwhile recommendation' (1972: 24).[9] Taxes are not only too high—and apparently especially those in the higher income brackets—but moreover, the TCC is of the opinion that they seem to be specially directed towards merchants and industrialists. Thus, the second line of defence takes shape. The reasoning is, if high taxes, etc. are unavoidable, an exception should be made for entrepreneurs such as those in the TCC. Its members, it was voiced, are entrepreneurs who hold special positions: they export and bring in hard currency. These members represent vulnerable companies and have enough trouble keeping their international competitive position. Moreover, they represent Kerala State, a state which is already 'forgotten' within India.

Reasoning along such lines, the TCC tried to get concessional tariffs regarding taxes and duties. In 1949 and 1950 complaints were made against taxation of foreign trade (1949: 11-12; 1950: 19-20); in 1952 taxes on rubber production—a 'strategic material' , the production of which is 'in the interest of the country as a whole' (1952: 16). In 1953 President Sulaiman Sait requested concessions to those branches in trade and industry that contribute substantially to the national income (1953: 17). In 1995 the same president applied for fiscal facilities for coir exports: 'Coir is the mainstay of a very large section of the population inhabiting the State and it is from this widely spread cottage industry that many eke out their living' (1955: 17).

In 1956 copra and coconut oil received special attention for concessions (1956: 17), and in 1957 it was again the turn of the 'plantation industries'. High taxes: 'naturally affect the industry's ability to earn foreign exchange which is so vitally needed' (1957: 15). Rubber was brought to the fore again in 1958 (1958: 16). Amelioration of sales tax was subsequently pleaded in 1963, in 1965 ('the vexed question of Sales Tax', 1965: 17), in 1971 and 1972.

Another argument that was often used by the TCC to claim tax and duty concessions was that Kerala (or Travancore-Cochin) contributed much to India's export earnings and should get more in return from the central government. The reasoning was that Kerala forms only 1 per cent of the national territory, is inhabited by four per cent of the national population, but contributed no less than 10 to 14 per cent of foreign earnings (1957: 19; 1961: 18; 1963: 13; 1968: 19). Thus, Kerala delivers much and gets little in return.

It is not surprising that the Chamber resisted the implementation of several aspects of labour legislation. The introduction of a national and compulsory provident fund, e.g., was opposed for the coir industry, a 'sick industry'. A provident fund, it was argued, will not benefit labourers but it will promote the closure of units and increase unemployment (1963: 16). On similar grounds the right to dismiss labourers at will ('when necessary') was defended (1949: 18-19), while a request was made not to apply the minimum wage regulations, as laid down in 1966 for port workers, to minor ports such as Alleppey (1966: 21).

A third line of defence was related to the speed with which changes of a fiscal and socio-economic nature were introduced. Laws are coming 'too soon and out of step with industrial progress', remarked Hann in 1950 (1950: 17). Hann returned to this issue in 1951 as he complained that the 'business executive' and the 'senior personnel' must devote the greater part of their time to study the new and changed rules in order that they do not offend them (1951: 17-18). In 1957 this complaint was repeated in extenso:

> Willing as we are to accept the change, it is unfortunate that the speed of legislation and the pace at which reforms are being carried out and the rush of execution of programmes and policies are so baffling that we have been given no time whatsoever to adjust ourselves to and be prepared for this big change. (1957: 14)

Obviously, the call for 'rest' was heard often in the annual speeches.

In addition to the three lines of open defence, an escape line has to be added. Occasional references have been made to illegal reactions against fiscal and similar measures, threatening the profitability of enterprises. Although these references are not direct, they are clear enough. The 'law abiding business executives', as several presidents described the TCC members,'. . . will gladly pay all taxes to government under the law without any evasion (1961: 16), but in 1964 Sulaiman Sait concluded that the honest taxpayer is frustrated and forced to close his enterprise (1964: 15). There were probably few honest taxpayers among the TCC members, as in 1972, President George went to great lengths to explain to the members that tax evasion (or rather the temptation to evade) would be much less if the taxpayer had confidence in the ways taxes were used (i.e., for 'really constructive purposes', whatever that might be), and less would be spent on a corrupt government machinery. He added, to make his position completely clear, that very few people would be able to resist the temptation to evade (1972: 24-5). It seems therefore that the TCC members found an effective counter-strategy against attacks on their profits, probably a more effective one than complaints and open protests.

Development Policies

Comments made by TCC presidents with regard to central government policies for developing India (by means of five-year plans) have been brought together under this heading. What matters here are the opinions about how India spent money—inclusive of the money from the Alleppey 'business executive'. In accordance with the optimistic expectation of the Chamber on the occasion of India's independence and its merger with Travancore, as early as 1948 President Cass spoke of the necessity of 'positive economic planning' by the government in order to explore and to exploit in an optimal way the natural resources, trade and industry (1948: 15).

Such a statement may seem surprising for a British entrepreneur of those days, but it should be remembered that 'planning' as a policy instrument of the government was already widely accepted in the later years of colonial rule. Within the Congress movement similar thoughts prevailed and were considered as a matter of fact after 1947. Also, among sectors of society such as trade unions and industrialists, the idea of 'planning' was accepted, though naturally with varying opinions about its contents.

The First Five-Year Plan (1951-6) has been considered as a hotchpotch of varying interests as far as the contents and the strategy of development planning went. By and large it has been described as friendly to the 'business executive', and therefore the expectations of Cass from 1948 came true. And even five year later, Sulaiman Sait could say: 'The Five-Year Plan is still our hope' (1953: 16). Yet the optimism about the five-year plans was not complete. Cass warned even in 1949 against 'idealistic schemes', which were more fitting for a country of millionaires, than for a land 'stricken with poverty as a result of the war' (1949: 66). The warnings and criticisms grew stronger from the mid-1950s on. Repeatedly the potentially important role of entrepreneurs was stressed, provided this role would become acknowledged among the planners. In 1955—at the closure of the first plan and during the preparations for the second, Sulaiman Sait remarked that free enterprise was not necessarily based on exploitation, nor public intervention in economic developments necessarily geared towards social justice (1955: 16).

In 1956 the Second Five-Year Plan was approved on a national level and President Sulaiman Sait was already in a dark mood about it in 1956. Its tone, according to the President, suggested heavy influences by commitments of the Congress party, the executive and parliament on the future course of India's development path towards a 'socialistic pattern of society', in which state involvement in many spheres of life would play a central role. According to Sulaiman Sait state interference should be restricted to basic economic sectors (like heavy industries, rail transport, etc.) and to those sectors in which private enterprise was weak. This approach, called the 'socialisation of the vacuum' was apparently seen by the TCC as a model for subsequent plans. But the second plan went far beyond this modest aim. Mind you for nationalizations, argued Sulaiman Sait, 'knowledgeable people' are of the opinion that bureaucrats operate slowly and fearfully, in contrast to entrepreneurs in the private sector (1956: 11-14). In 1957 Sulaiman Sait repeated his comments: he appealed to the central government to have trust in the 'business executive' in order to gain his wholehearted co-operation in fulfilling the second plan (1957: 13-4).

The great change took place in 1958. The second plan was not sufficiently covered by incomes and will thus lead to increasing tax pressure, argued Sulaiman Sait. He was apparently 'angry' when he commented on it. India should certainly have a 'plan' in order to make progress, he remarked:

> But we seem to have instead an unplanned expenditure which has unleashed inflationary forces to the utter detriment of our general economy and the ultimate objectives of economic progress. That is the tragedy of current politics. (1957-8: 13)

Similar criticisms were raised against the Third Five-Year Plan (1961-6). The 'ideological' character of it was attacked as being unrealistic for Indian conditions, and again the entrepreneurs of Alleppey pointed out their preferred alternative by remarking: 'We merchants have no ideology' (1963: 13). In 1964—the last year of Sulaiman Sait's long-lasting presidency of the TCC—the opposition against 'the plan' was possibly even fiercer. Sulaiman Sait advocated a 'plan holiday' and rethinking of future planning (1964: 12). His successor, Joseph continued along the same line: development should be more modest and less demanding on the taxpayer; it should exert less *dirigisme* and leave more opportunities for the market sector.

After 1966 the Chamber presidents did not anymore talk much about the nature of development planning. They occasionally discussed some details, as President Mathew did in his annual speech about missing roads and bridges across the backwaters: 'But when the road to the East will be there, a short connection with the rich hinterland is restored, and there is no doubt that the completion of these bridges will give a big boost to export traffic' (TCC 1973: 27), but steered away from any political opposition to India's development. Also, in this sector of TCC reactions, it seems that the period till about 1950 can be characterized as somewhat optimistic, while 'protests' dominated between 1950 and about 1965. Silence governed afterwards.

VIEWS OF THE CHAMBER: 'ITS' TOWN

The closest ring around the TCC consists of the conglomerate of local facilities and local conditions which should serve the entrepreneurial interests. One might say that Alleppey 'belonged' to the Chamber from the point of view of its members. Labourers should obey and infrastructure should be oriented toward the superior position and activities of international trade, represented by the members of the TCC. Of course, Alleppey cannot be separated from Travancore, Kerala or India in the sense that many developments and decisions originating elsewhere, had their impact on the local society. But for pragmatic reasons some sort of local sector has been carved out: a series of developments and conditions that have affected local society in particular, such as the functioning of the port, the (lack of) roads to the hinterland, local trade union politics, etc.

Labour, Labourers, Labour Unions, Labour-Unrest

In preceding sections protests against labour legislation have been mentioned. This legislation did not come out of the blue: it was secured by organized labour. Moreover, unions have been active in implementing the legislation, with varying degrees of success. In Travancore-Cochin and in Kerala implementation was intensively enforced, compared to most other Indian states. The same holds true for Alleppey, compared to many other towns in Travancore (-Cochin) and in Kerala. The earliest trade unions in Travancore started in Alleppey in the early 1920s, while organized labour became a serious political force from the late 1930s onwards (see Chapter 4). Travancore state, however, committed itself sufficiently to employers' interests in order not to arouse feelings of uneasiness among the members of the TCC. President Cass recalled, e.g. the Punnapra-Vayalar uprising in 1946 as follows: 'There were signs of serious trouble in September last and we are thankful to government for the firm steps they took to keep the situation under control' (1947: 19).

However, since late 1940s an explosive social climate reigned in Alleppey. Mobilized and organized labourers were no longer (or at any rate less) oppressed by the state and saw their chances to realize long-standing demands regarding wages and other labour conditions. Employers resisted but learned by experience that India was different from Travancore. Mediation and arbitration took the place of *lathi*-charges and machine guns. Besides the activities of organized labour itself, it is this institutionalized form of arbitration of labour disputes through the installed Industrial Tribunals which has been a source of wrath to the Chamber.

Comments on labour union activities has been negative as may be expected. However, the Chamber made a clear distinction between labourers and their leaders, and especially the latter were distrusted. As early as 1947 Cass observed that 'responsible leadership' is essential: 'it is too easy to start a labour movement, but very difficult to control it once started' (1947: 19) and he added that many of the labour-leaders came from outside the factories, without any intimate knowledge of local circumstances. In a similar way Hann spoke about 'rank indiscipline on the factory floors', '. . . made worse by "leaders" exploiting labour for their own ends. Integrity and discipline are among the casualties of the last war' (1951: 15). Sulaiman Sait continued in 1957. He accused trade union leaders of starting their careers on the backs of the workers and employers. Moreover, he related trade union activities to those of political parties and hence to state power. It is not accidental that Sulaiman Sait made this accusation exactly in 1957, as the first communist ministry in Kerla was installed in this year. Sulaiman Sait went on pointing out linkages by complaining about police behaviour—now under the command of a communist minister. He expected police action against anti-social elements in the state who operate 'on the borderline of industrial dispute and breach of the peace' (1957: 17).

The TCC had to prepare for more shocking events—and for the forceful criticism of Sulaiman Sait. This president spoke about, labour orgies (1958: 14), while in the same year he started to address his fellow members in the following way:

> When I think of addressing you this time, I almost quail under a deep sense of chagrin and frustration and wish, therefore, to make my speech very brief indeed. (1958: 12)

Occasionally, the tone was milder and more subdued. President Prabhakaran spoke about: 'Unfortunately a few incidents here and there' (1968: 20), when discussing labour relations, but it should not be forgotten that among his listeners was the minister of industry as a guest of honour. And this guest was no less that T.V. Thomas, a trade-union leader and CPI politician from Alleppey and one of the bitter opponents of the entrepreneurial class and its practices, but now minister in the second communist ministry in Kerala (the United Front Government of 1967-9). In the following year—and without any attending communist minister—Joseph picked up Sulaiman Sait's approach. He spoke about 'frivolous and irresponsible strikes' (1969: 17-18), while President George discussed the 'violent and vulgar' nature of a strike of headload workers (1972: 28). On the other hand, several presidents pleaded for an armistice between labourers and employers, 'a statewide industrial truce' for at last five years (1968: 20; repeated in 1969: 18) or for ten years (1970: 17).

But, in the early 1970s a distinction was again made between 'good' labourers and 'bad' leaders, like Cass and Hann did some twenty to twenty-five years before. The energy of the mass of enlightened labourers requires steering in a constructive direction, according to President Karuna Karan (1971: 18-19).

The Urban Infrastructure: All Roads Lead to Chamber Road

The TCC headquarters are located at the corner of Chamber Road and Commercial Canal, in Factory Ward. From the building the neglected canal can be seen, as well as the worn-out tar on Chamber Road. A few hundred yards to the west the shaky port equipment rusts away, and empty godowns and factory sheds surround the premises of the Chamber. Though the building is new (1971), the TCC falls in line with the desolate atmosphere of the surrounding area. Its income had declined because it originates to a fair extent from 'weighing fees' and similar services to businesses. Its staff has been decimated. Several presidents refer to the 'skeleton staff' of the Chamber during the 1970s: a full-time secretary and a few peons and clerks.

It is no wonder that many presidents—normally at the end of their speeches—called attention to the deterioration of the level of services that could be offered to trade and industry. A wide variety of topics have been covered in this respect: the poor functioning of the port was a major one, of course. A new tug was needed, a new crane should come, more lighters were needed. President Chandrakumar L. Palicha, noted even in 1979 that ad hoc measures for a functioning port were taken, but: 'I regret to state that no permanent arrangements have been made as yet by the authorities to use this port' (1979: 14).

Similarly, the conditions of the canals were criticized: too shallow and overgrown with weeds. The inadequate level of other facilities was discussed, like the poor condition of roads, or the lack of any roads (or railroad) at all. A major pride of Alleppey, its telephone network—the first in Travancore—functioned inadequately, which made President Joseph remark sarcastically: What else can we expect under 'nationalization' (1965: 19). This list can be extended to several pages of comments.

But decay and negligence compete with redundancy in Alleppey, in Factory Ward and elsewhere. The neglected watersides of the canals, occasionally used as a refuse dump, have also become rather useless, as few *vellam* with cargo need these for unloading. The shallow canals are empty, the cranes not only rusty, but idle as well.

THE TRAVANCORE CHAMBER OF COMMERCE, FROM 'OWNER' OF 'ALLEPPEY PVT. LTD.', TO INVESTOR IN SURVIVAL STRATEGIES

The TCC has experienced a dramatic period in its existence, from 1947 onwards. It had been an organization of a powerful economic elite, and it became one of just a couple of owners of enterprises. Some standing for past glories, others just being local entrepreneurs. As champions of (profitable) free trade, its members had to submit to state interference in their dealings. As capitalist entrepreneurs—and owners and commanders of scarce capital and scarce access to a wider consuming world—they had to acknowledge the power of 'labour', notwithstanding its abundance and hence 'low value' in the eyes of the business executives. Moreover, the economic base of business prosperity fell away: in general, the demand from overseas for coir ceased. The TCC had known Alleppey as a spider in a network of waterways, full of loaded boats. Now they saw the town isolated and bereft of many of its backward and forward linkages: roads and railroads avoided the town; these carried wagons and trucks with cargo to other, better ports.

The foregoing sections witness the assumed equation of TCC opinions and wider local interests. The Chamber tended to identify itself with Alleppey at large. Were the presidents aware of the negative effects on 'business' during the late 1940s, the 1950s, 1960s and 1970s? To some extent they were, of course, and their protests and complaints, examples of which have been recorded here, bear witness to this. But yet it seems that the tone of the annual speeches implied temporary setbacks to business, which could be overcome. This may indicate a certain dualism. On the one hand, the yardstick used by the presidents to evaluate the present was the past. On the other, nowadays survival played a central role. During some years survival seemed to be pursued by protests, but afterwards 'silence' was chosen, 'keeping out of trouble'. From studies on entrepreneurial elite in India, Panini concluded that: 'the adapted qualities of India's entrepreneurs to the changing economic and social milieu' are outspoken (1978: 91). Adaptation has, however, often been employed as a prerequisite for climbing social ladders. The Alleppey entrepreneurs, on the other hand, had to take care not to fall, or not to fall too far. By and large, most of them succeeded (see also Chapter 7) though they had to disguise their survival carefully. One may wonder, finally, whether a strategy of a silent survival would work, or whether the erstwhile mighty lobby of the elitist TCC will die as an outdated relic of former times in Alleppey.

NOTES

1. In 1953 a 'gentlemen's agreement' was reached, which included that during alternate years the chairmanship should be held by one of the European members of the chamber (Annual report 1952-3: 19). The first Travancorean president A. R. Sulaiman Sait, who succeeded the Briton Smith who was ill, was replaced by Smith again. But in 1955 this rule was once more changed and Sulaiman Sait remained president till 1964, assisted till the end of 1955 by a British vice-president.
2. The Swiss representatives in the Chamber had apparently taken positions different from the British ones. In many lists they were mentioned last, after British and Indians. In the Committee they did not play an important role.
3. This departure can be related to the agreement between the Indian government and the All-India Associated Chambers of Commerce, in 1960. This agreement included the codicil that executive positions in foreign companies had to be 'Indianized' at high speed (see Kuchal, 1972: 365).
4. No information about membership was available for the years after 1974.
5. The annual reports, the contents of which will be quoted often in this chapter, have been referred to by the final (half-)year of reporting, and not by the formal year of publication. Often a year of publication is not given.
6. The leader of the CPI in Kerala, E.M.S. Namboodiripad declared shortly after the communist victory that the new government would choose a path to promote industrial progress in the state 'businessmen and traders would be encouraged, but at the same time he would curb their tendency to excess profiteering. His government was not averse to industrialists making reasonable profits and promoted the coming in of any capital, including American capital, provided it came in on reasonable terms.' The new Minister for industries,

K.P. Gopalan added that the industrialists would get a 'reasonable profit, the workers would get a reasonable share of the profit' quoted by Lieten, 1980: 60.

7. National and state taxes together only contributed 6.7 per cent to the national income in 1950-1, while fifteen years later this share had risen to 14.8 per cent. Indirect taxes especially were raised in that period. In 1965-6 indirect taxes contributed 60 per cent of tax income, against 35 per cent in 1950-1. Malenbaum, from whom these figures have been taken, describes the system of taxation as more and more regressive, i.e. more and more oppressive to the poor (1971: 77-8).
8. The Factory Acts (1934, 1948, 1954) deal with those industrial companies with ten or more labourers, or twenty or more if no source of inanimate power is applied. In it elaborate provisions have been laid down regarding labour conditions: working hours for men, women, and children; leave; illness; etc. It should be added that legislation and implementation are not one and the same.
9. I do not have the income tax rates of 1971-2 available, but based on data for 1967-8 it is seen that the highest income-bracket starts at annual tax income of Rs. 70,000 (taken from a leaflet: You and your income tax, 1967-8). For the sake of comparison, the rural poverty-line was drawn at an annual per capita income of Rs. 216 by the influential economist Ohja (1971).

EPILOGUE

CHAPTER 10

From Alleppey back to Alappuzha

FROM ALLEPPEY TO ALAPPUZHA

When—in 1762—Travancore's Chief Minister Kesava Das decided to start a seaport for the profitable export of the 'wealth of Travancore', he chose to have this outlet at a village in the north of the state: Alappuzha. Its convenient site, that of a spider in a web of inland waterways, and near to the coast and the Arabian Sea was an acknowledgement of a natural asset of the village: its physical-geographical location. He added another asset: state protection and state promotion of the new seaport, which became operational in the late 1770s and soon got the 'easy' name Alleppey. These assets appeared to be time-bound. The protection of Alleppey's export trade was first withdrawn in the 1860 as 'free trade' was the buzzword of British India that reached beyond its directly controlled parts of the subcontinent into the many pseudo-independent princely states such as Travancore. Free trade, however, appeared an impetus for economic growth, then and there, and Alleppey moreover acquired a new and powerful asset: the industrial production and overseas shipping of coir products. This formed a new material base for an unforeseen economic expansion. At the same time it became the cradle of a self-conscious and politically aware labour force. This force mattered, despite strong counterforces by 'vested interests', and resulted in a growing polarization between traditional elites and coming on labourers. This force transformed Kerala into a state that heard labourers' demands for less exploitation, though too often it was not accompanied by better material prospects.

Next to the withdrawal of the asset of state protection of Alleppey's export trade, a second withdrawal of one of Alleppey's assets took more time. The state of Travancore did not honour anymore Alleppey's physical-geographical location. Since late 1800 roads far from Alleppey, but reaching Cochin and other ports were constructed, a railroad as far from Alleppey but as emphatically pointing at Cochin, became operational in 1956. Moreover, Travancore decided in the 1890s that the port of Alleppey could not become a viable proposition for future marine transport and supported the civil engineering works to create the modern, full-fledged port of Cochin, which was opened in 1928. Alleppey remained crippled but became finally empty-handed when the town—or rather the local population and the local society—largely lost its final asset, which it had seen in its midst since 1859. The industrial production and provision of finished coir products, rope, mats, and mattings to consumers all over the world came largely to an end in the 1970s, apart from household-scale activities.

Sadly enough, the local society found consolation in the collectively felt neglect by the outer world, be that world located in the capital of Travancore or that of India. The non-provision of a railway, linking Alleppey with that outer (and seemingly profitable) world functioned as a super-structural asset and a blessing in disguise for many citizens: a common longing and easy scapegoat, as I mentioned earlier. But then, the railway was sanctioned in 1979, 'promised' wrote the daily *The Hindu* (Figure 10.1), and indeed, in 1989 the first trains connected Alleppey with Cochin, and subsequently Alleppey with the south: Kollam and Thiruvananthapuram, three years later. Even the asset of a common longing was no more when the trains just rode.

It was hence that the assets that made Alappuzha into Alleppey, and made Alleppey have its momentous history, were outdated and gone. Why keeping hence that name of a lazy corrosion of the name of a fishing village with a few black-

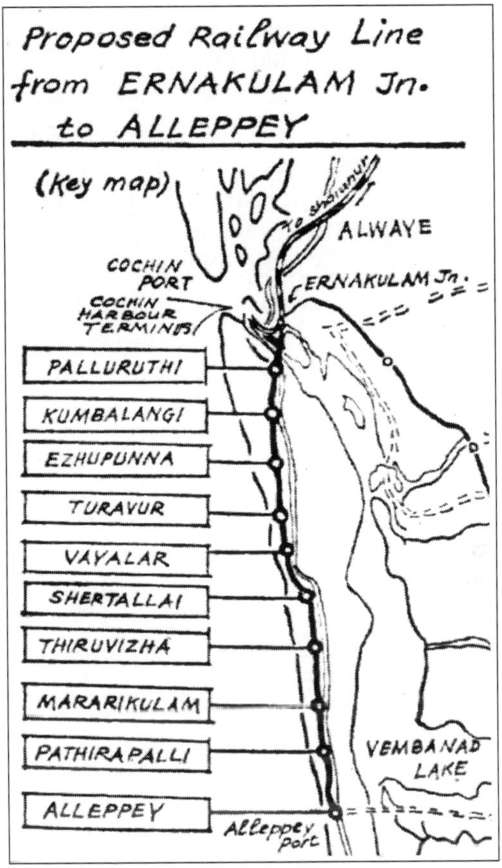

Figure 10.1: The proposed railway, *The Hindu*, 13 February 1979

smiths? Why not returning to the original? It required a formal act to erase the rusty, faded, assets by the 1980s of Alleppey. This happened in 2012 when the municipal council decided to rename Alleppey into Alappuzha.

ALAPPUZHA

Alleppey lasted 200 odd years. The formal decision to rename Alleppey into Alappusha brought a new reality to the fore. A reality of a strong labour force for which employment was scarce. Some labourers found jobs in the Gulf, as so many others from Kerala. Others became engaged in the re-invented asset of the backwaters. Where in the past *vellam* loaded with pepper or coir yarn and poled by strong Ezhavas found their ways to the quays of Commercial Canal, now houseboats glide through the alleys of the backwaters. They carry tourists and make the outcry by some in the past that tourism will be the future golden asset of Alappuzha real. Will Alappuzha become the 'Venice of the East'? Its over 1,000 houseboats ply now the backwaters and penetrate deep into the town via its canals. But what is the environmental impact of this new tourism? Who will profit, who has to pay? The story of Alappuzha has to be written in the future and even a start—on tourism and on so many other relevant items—should not (and cannot) be put on paper here.

APPENDIX

TABLE 1: STATISTICS OF SHIPPING AT ALLEPPEY, 1870-1 TO 1899-1900

Year	*Number of Ships*		*Tonnage of Ships*		*Tonnage/ship*	*Tonnage/steamer*	*Source:*
	All Ships	*Steamers*	*All Ships* × *1,000*	*Steamers* × *1,000*		*RAT*	
1870-1	–	–	–	–	–	–	
1871-2	343	50	77	–	225	–	
1872-3	338	53	78	–	231	–	
1873-4	345	50	63	272	183	544	
1874-5	313	86	98	625	313	727	
1875-6	358	90	98	572	273	636	
1876-7	266	84	77	492	289	586	
1877-8	299	109	148	1,179	494	1,082	
1878-9	371	110	161	1,290	434	1,173	
1879-80	282	–	177	–	628	–	
1880-1	–	–	173	–	–	–	
1881-2	310	–	–	–	–	–	
1882-3	332	–	186	–	561	–	
1883-4	426	–	216	–	506	–	
1884-5	401	–	199	–	495	–	
1885-6	453	–	248	–	548	–	
1886-7	428	–	252	–	589	–	

Contd.

TABLE 1: *Contd.*

Year	*Number of Ships*		*Tonnage of Ships*		*Tonnage/ship*	*Tonnage/steamer*	*Source: RAT*
	All Ships	*Steamers*	*All Ships × 1,000*	*Steamers × 1,000*			
1887-8	435	174	292	–	671	–	
1888-9	430	169	259	–	603	–	
1889-90	414	–	270	–	651	–	
1890-1	490	–	342	–	697	–	
1891-2	397	–	300	–	755	–	
1992-3	–	–	–	–	–	–	
1993-4	411	–	347	–	843	–	
1894-5	416	–	316	–	760	–	
1895-6	360	–	288	–	801	–	
1896-7	309	–	245	–	792	–	
1897-8	328	–	297	–	904	–	
1898-9	366	–	300	–	820	–	
1899-1900	265	–	248	–	838	–	

Source: RAT.

TABLE 2: STATISTICS OF SHIPPING AT ALLEPPEY, 1915-16 TO 1939-40

Year	*Number of all Ships*	*Number of Steamers*	*Tonnage of all Ships × 1,000*	*Tonnage per Ship*
1915-16	–	–	–	–
1916-17	–	23	88	–
1917-18	–	12	69	–
1918-19	–	–	–	–
1919-20	–	–	–	–
1920-1	–	82	179	–
1921-2	–	110	311	–
1922-3	–	152	426	–
1923-4	246	175	441	1,793
1924-5	288	242	550	1,910
1925-6	294	269	624	2,122
1926-7	348	307	715	2,054
1927-8	447	342	778	1,740
1928-9	572	420	940	1,643
1929-30	681	450	1,046	1,536
1930-1	601	438	1,035	1,722
1931-2	603	429	1,014	1,681
1932-3	550	425	1,027	1,867
1933-4	394	384	914	2,320
1934-5	550	386	941	1,695
1935-6	477	415	946	1,983
1936-7	425	348	817	1,922
1937-8	442	357	892	2,018
1938-9	397	368	958	2,413
1939-40	256	220	524	2,048

Source: RAT/TAR.

TABLE 3: STATISTICS OF SHIPPING AT ALLEPPEY
1940-1 TO 1973-4

Year	*Number of all Ships*	*Number of Steamers*	*Tonnage of all Ships*	*Tonnage per Ship*
1940-1	171	108	238.000	1,390
1941-2	99	18	49.000	498
1942-3	175	–	12.000	70
1943-4	332	1	29.000	87
1944-5	255	25	29.000	112
1945-6	224	41	72.000	321
1946-7	110	81	127.000	1,157
1947-8	188	110	198.000	1,584
1948-9	174	142	450.000	2,585
1949-50	236	202	509.000	2,155
1950-1	186	150	424.000	2,277
1951-2	121	109	305.000	2,520
1952-3	176	134	416.000	2,362
1953-4	151	120	504.000	3,339
1954-5	158	131	552.000	3,492
1955-6	124	104	457.000	3,682
1956-7	116	99	406.000	3,501
1957-8	147	149	570.000	3,878
1958-9	191	185	715.000	3,746
1959-60	202	183	757.000	3,745
1960-1	170	157	567.000	3,335
1961-2	156	153	651.000	4,173
1962-3	150	145	635.000	4,235
1963-4	130	130	561.000	4,317
1964-5	121	121	508.000	4,716
1965-6	101	101	424.000	4,203
1966-7	99	99	431.000	4,350
1967-8	102	102	436.000	4,273
1968-9	90	90	385.000	4,274
1969-70	64	64	309.000	4,827
1970-1	40	40	178.000	4,457
1971-2	39	36	121.000	3,122
1972-3	31	31	133.000	4,286
1973-4	16	16	58.000	3,632

Source: TCC Tonnage (all ships) figures rounded.

TABLE 4: COIR EXPORTS, KERALA PORTS, 1951-2 TO 1969-70

Year	*Unfinished Coir Goods × 1,000 tons*				*Finished Coir Goods × 1,000 tons*			
	Cochin	*Calicut*	*Alleppey*	*Total*	*Cochin*	*Calicut*	*Alleppey*	*Total*
1951-2	32	6	6	44	10	0	NA	NA
1952-3	38	4	9	51	10	0	NA	NA
1953-4	40	9	7	56	11	NA	NA	NA
1954-5	39	10	7	56	12	NA	NA	NA
1955-6	40	8	7	55	11	NA	NA	NA
1956-7	43	4	11	58	11	0	8	19
1957-8	33	7	12	51	10	0	8	18
1958-9	30	8	14	52	12	1	7	20
1959-60	32	7	13	53	11	1	7	29
1960-1	29	6	12	48	10	1	6	18
1961-2	32	6	17	56	11	1	5	16
1962-3	32	6	18	56	11	1	6	17
1963-4	35	5	16	56	13	0	6	20
1964-5	34	4	14	53	14	0	5	18
1965-6	28	3	15	46	13	0	4	17
1966-7	27	2	14	43	14	0	4	18
1967-8	30	2	13	45	13	0	4	17
1968-9	23	2	15	40	12	0	3	16
1969-70	24	1	11	35	14	0	2	17

Sources: GoK 1972, TCC. Tonnage figures rounded.

TABLE 5: POPULATION PER WARD, CENSUS OF 1971

Ward	*Population*	*inh./ha*	*Ward*	*Population*	*inh./ha*
1. Kalarcode	7,167	9	17. Market	3,967	110
2. Pazhaveedu	5,737	39	18. Factory	3,105	44
3. Vattayl-Vadakkal	10,729	38	19. Seaview	3,578	60
4. Kuthiranpanthy	5,009	35	20. Shertallai Canal	4,832	89
5. Beach	6,194	86	21. Power house	4,153	94
6. Zakaria Bazar	5,220	54	22. Sanathanam	5,097	78
7. Lainath	5,103	116	23. Zilla court	4,618	50
8. Allicherry	3,614	77	24. Kanjiramchira	3,820	87
9. Vellakinar	2,576	76	25. Thumbolly	4,911	27
10. Puthanangady	3,630	101	26. Aruttavazhi	4,803	48
11. Municipal Office	3,417	55	27. Kommady	3,319	41
12. Palace	3,207	52	28. Poonthoppu	4,914	46
13. Thiruvampady	4,119	63	29. Thondankulangara	5,030	8
14. Chungam	5,915	38	30. Asramam	5,096	53
15. Thirumala	2,568	45	31. Avalakunnu-Thothampally	10,381	33
16. Mullakkal	3,285	75	32. Kottaankulangara	6,588	25
			33. Nehru Trophy	4,464	6

Source: Census of India 1971, 1973.

Bibliography

SERIES

RAT, Government of Travancore, Report on the Administration of Travancore, for the administrative years 1865-6 (Malayam Era 1041) to 1924-5 (ME 1100). Not consulted (missing at the India Office Library and Records, London): 1898-9; 1900-1901; 1902-3; 1905-6; 1906-7; 1907-8; 1908-9; 1912-13; 1914-15; 1915-16; 1920-1.

TAR, Travancore Administration Report, consulted for the years 1925-6 (ME 1101) to 1942-3 (ME 1118).

TCC, Travancore Chamber of Commerce, The annual reports of the Chamber from 1946-7 to 1973-4 have been consulted.

SOURCES PUBLISHED IN ALLEPPEY

Kalathil, Abraham, 1979, Letter to the Editor on the coastal railway, *Indian Express*, 28 February.

Koya, Noorudeen, 1976, Alleppey Town: Looking Back, in *Munnani*, 23 August.

Nair, Narayanan , (advocate), 1971, Labour Problems and Development of Alleppey Town, Paper presented at the Seminar on development of Alleppey town, 29 May.

Nair, J.S., (President, All-Kerala Railway Users Association), 1979, Leeding Light in Progress, speech delivered on the occasion of the inauguration of the construction of the railway-line Alleppey-Cochin, 15 April 1979.

Parthasarathy, K., 1967, Alleppey, the Venice of the East, in, *Boat Race Souvenir.*

Pilla, Omana, 1966, Alleppey Cochin Railway, Memorandum to the minister of railways, Government of India.

Pilla, Omana, 1971, The Development of Alleppey, Paper presented at the Seminar on the development of Alleppey town, 29 May.

Pramani, Loovis, 1971, What happened in Punnapra, in, *Punnapra-Vayalar Silver Jubilee Souvenir.*

Prasad, P.P. (State port officer, marine adviser Government of Kerala) 1971, Improvement of Alleppey Port, Paper presented at the Seminar on development of Alleppey town, 29 May.

Varghese, Mathew (Chief town planner, Government of Kerala), 1971, Alleppey Town, Development Prospects. Paper presented at the Seminar on development of Alleppey town, 29 May.

Unsigned articles in: *Indian Express*, *Munnani*.

OTHER SOURCES

Aiya, V. Nagam, 1906, *The Travancore State Manual*, Three volumes, Trivandrum.

Alleppey Municipal Council, n.d., *Administration Report for 1974-5*, Alleppey.

Ansari, J., H., 1969, A Study of Settlement Pattern in Kerala, in, *Urban and Rural Planning Thoughts*, vol. XII, pp. 101-62.

Bayly, Susan, 1984, Hindu Kingship and the Origin of Community: Religion, State and Society in Kerala, *1750-1850*, in, *Modern Asian Studies*, vol. 18, pp. 177-213.

Bernard, K. L., 1977, *Flashes of Kerala History*, Cochin.

Bhaskaran, N. K., 1984, Social Reform Movements and Politics in Kerala, in, *Journal of Kerala Studies*, vol. XI, parts 1-4, pp. 205-28.

Bristow, Sir Robert, 1959, *Cochin Saga, A History of Foreign Government and Business Adventures in Kerala, South India, by Arabs, Romans, Venetians, Dutch and British, together with the Personal Narrative of the Last Adventurer and an Epilogue*. Paico Publishing House, Ernakulam-Cochin.

Census of India 1901, 1903, vol. XXVI, *Travancore*, Part 1, Report; Part II, Imperial Tables; Part III, Provincial Tables, Trivandrum.

——, 1911, 1912, vol. XXIII, *Travancore*, Part I, Report, Part I, Imperial Tables, Trivandrum.

——, 1921, 1922, vol. XXV, *Travancore*, Part 1, Report, Part II, Imperial Tables, Trivandrum.

——, 1931, 1932, vol. XXVIII, *Travancore*. Part I, Report, Part II, Imperial Table, Trivandrum

——, 1931, 1933, vol. XXI, *Cochin*, Ernakulam.

——, 1941, 1942, vol. XXV, *Travancore*, Part I Report, Part II Imperial Tables, Part III, State Tables, Trivandrum.

——, 1951, 1953, vol. XIII, *Travancore-Cochin*, Part I, report, Part II Tables, Delhi.

——, 1961, 1964, vol. VII, *Kerala*, Part VII-A, *Selected Crafts of Kerala*, Delhi.

——, 1971, 1973, Series 9, *Kerala, District Census Handbook.*

Census of Travancore 1891, 1894, *Report on the Census of Travancore taken by command of His Highness the Maharajah on the 27 February, 1891*, Madras.

Charlesworth, N., 1982, *British Rule and the Indian Economy 1800-1914*, McMillan, London.

Coir Board, 1963, *Report on the Economic and Statistical Survey of Coir Industry 1960*, Ernakulam (co-published in Coir Economics and Statistics, vol. IV, nr. 2, July 1962).

Das Gupta, A., 1967, *Malabar in Asian trade, 1740-1800*, Cambridge University Press, Cambridge.

Davey, G.H., n.d., *Reminiscences of James Darragh & Henry Smail*, Typescript, n.p.

Dutt, Ashok K., 1983, Cities of South Asia, in Stanly D. Brunn & Jack F. Williams, *Cities of the World*, New York.

Fonseca, R., 1969, The Walled City of Old Delhi, in P. Oliver, ed., *Shelter and Society*, Barrie & Jenkins, London.

Fuller, C. J., 1976, Kerala Christians and the Caste System, *Man* (New Series), vol. II, nr. 1.

Gadgil, D.R., 1971, *The Industrial Evolution of India in Recent Times 1860-1939* (fifth edition), Bombay.

Government of Kerala, 1966 (Department of Town Planning and Architecture), *Development Plan for Alleppey Town*, Trivandrum, 1966.

Government of Kerala, 1972, *Statistics for Planning, Series 10, Export and Import Statistics*, Trivandrum

Government of Kerala, 1974, *Report on Kuttanad Development Project.* N.P.

Government of Kerala, 1975, *Alleppey District Gazetteer*, Trivandrum.

Government of Travancore-Cochin, 1955, *Report of the Committee on Coir Mats and Matting Manufacturing Industry* (Chairman: G. Parameswaran Pillai), Trivandrum.

Gulati, L., 1981, *Profiles in Female Poverty, a Study of Five Poor Working Women in Kerala*, Hindustan, Delhi.

Harrison, J.B., 1980, Allahabad, a Sanitary History, in Kenneth Ballhatchet & John Harrison (eds), *The City in South Asia, Pre-Modern and Modern*, Curzon Press, London, pp. 167-95.

Hatch, Emily Gilchriest, 1933, *Travancore, A Guidebook for the Visitor*, London.

Heller, Patrick, 1999, *The Labor of Development, Workers and the Transformation of Capitalism in Kerala, India*, Cornell University Pres, Ithaca and London.

Ibrahim, P., 1978, The Development of Transport Facilities in Kerala, a Historical Review, in *Social Scientist*, vol. 6, nr. 8 (March).

Isaac, T.M. Thomas, 1982, Class Struggle and Structural Change, Coir Mats and Matting Industry in Kerala, 1950-1980, in, *Economic and Political Weekly*, vol. XVII, nr. 31 (Review of Political Economy).

Isaac, T. M. Thomas, 1983, Class Struggle and Transition to Specifically Capitalist form of Production: Some Conclusions of a Study Tour of Coir Industry in Kerala, *Social Scientist*, vol. 11, nr. 12 (December).

Isaac, T.M. Thomas, 1985, From Caste Consciousness to Class Consciousness, Alleppey Coir Workers during Inter-war Period, in *Economic and Political Weekly*, vol. XX, nr. 4 (Review of Political Economy).

James, Rachel, 1981, *Casual Workers in the Cashew Industry, a Profile*. Interim Report nr. 10, Indo-Dutch Kerala research project, Centre for Anthropological and Sociological Studies, University of Amsterdam.

Jeffrey, Robin, 1976, *The Decline of Nayar Dominance, Society and Politics in Travancore, 1847-1908*, Sussex University Press, London.

Jeffrey, Robin, 1984, 'Destroy Capitalism', Growing Solidarity of Alleppey's Coir Workers, 1930-1940, in, *Economic and Political Weekly*, vol. XIX, nr. 29 (July), pp. 1159-66.

Kemp, T., 1978, *Historical Patterns of Industrialization*, Longman, London.

King, Anthony D., 1976, *Colonial Urban Development, Culture, Social Power and Environment*, Routledge & Kegan Paul, London.

Kooiman, D., 1983, Christelijke zending, sociale mobiliteit en geweld, een klerenconflict in Travancore, *Sociologische Gids*, Vl. XXX, nr. 5, pp. 351-373

Kuchhal, S.C., 1972, *The Industrial Economy of India*, Allahabad.

Kulkarni, M. R., 1971, *Industrial Development*. New Delhi.

Kusuman, K. K., 1973, *Slavery in Travancore*, Trivandrum.

Kusuman, K. K., 1977, *The Extremist Movement in Kerala*, Charithram Publications, Trivandrum.

Langley, W. K. M., n.d., *Century in Malabar, the history of Peirce, Leslie & Co. Ltd 1862-1962*, Madras.

Lemercinier, G., 1983, *Religion and Ideology in Kerala*, Louvain-La-Neuve.

Lewandowski, Susan, 1977, Changing Form and Function in the Ceremonial and the Colonial Port City in India: An Historical Analysis of Madurai and Madras, in *Modern Asian Studies*, Nr. 2, pp. 183-212.

Lewandowski, Susan, 1979, Changing Form and Function in the Ceremonial and the Port City in India: An Historical Analysis of Madurai and Madras, in, K.N. Chaudhuri & C.S. Dewy (eds), *Economy and Society, Essays in Indian Economic and Social History*, Delhi, pp. 299-330.

Lewandowski, Susan, 1983, The Built Environment and Cultural Symbolism in Post-colonial Madras, in John A. Agnew, John Mercer & David E. Sopher (eds), *The City in Cultural Context*, Boston, pp. 237-54.

Lieten, George Kristoffel, 1980, *The First Communist Ministry in Kerala, 1957-9*, Publication nr. 28, University of Amsterdam, Centre for the Study of Anthropology and Sociology, Department of South- and Southeast Asian Studies, Amsterdam

Malenbaum, W., 1971, *Modern India's Economy*, Merrill, Columbus (Ohio).

Mathew, Jibin, 2019, *Development of Transport and Communication in Travancore (1860-1948): The Socio-economic Impact*. Unpublished Thesis, Department of History, University of Calicut.

Meile, Pierre, 1939, La naissance d'un port: Cochin, in, *Annales de Géographie*, vol. XLVIII, pp. 276-85.

Menon, A Sreedhara, 1967, *A Survey of Kerala History*, Sahitya Pravathaka Cooperative Society, Ltd., Kottayam.

Mukerjee, Ramkrishna, 1974, *The Rise and Fall of the East India Company*, Monthly Review Press, New York, and London.

Namboodiripad, E.M.S., 1967, *Kerala, Yesterday, Today and Tomorrow*, Calcutta.

Nightingale, Pamela, 1970, *Trade and Empire in Western India, 1784-1806*, Cambridge University Press, Cambridge.

Ohja, P.D., 1971, A Configuration of Indian Poverty, in A.J. Fonseca (ed.), *Challenge of Poverty in India*, Vikas, Delhi.

Ouwerkerk, Louise, 1994, *No Elephants for the Maharaja, Social and Political Change in the Princely State of Travancore (1921-1947)*, edited with an Introduction by Dick Kooiman, Manohar, New Delhi.

Panini, M.N., 1978, Network and Styles: Industrial Entrepreneurs in Faridabad, in, S. Satish Saberwal (ed.), *Process and Institution in Urban India*, New Delhi.

Peruman, Nilkan, 1939, *The Truth About Travancore*, Madras.

Pillai, T.K. Veelu, 1935, *A History of Travancore*, Trivandrum.

Pillai, T.K. Veelu, 1940, *The Travancore State Manual*, 4 vols., Trivandrum.

Poonen, T. I., 1948, *A Survey of the Rise of the Dutch Power in Malabar (1603-78)*, University of Travancore, Trivandrum.

Poonen, T. I., 1978, *Dutch Hegemony in Malabar and Its Collapse*, University of Kerala, Trivandrum.

Prakash, B.A. 1977, Coir Manufacturing in the Doldrums, , *Social Scientist*, vol. 6, nr. 1 (August).

Prakash, B. A., 2018, *Economic History of Kerala from 1800 to 1947 AD, Part II: T. Travancore, Change in Agriculture, Industry, Transport, Power and Education*, Thiruvananthapuram Economic Studies Society,

Rajendran, N., 1979, *Establishment of British Power in Malabar (1664 to 1799)*, Allahabad.

Ramesh, A. & Allen G. Noble, 1977, Pattern and Process in South Indian Cities, in Allen G. Noble & Ashok K. Dutt (eds), *Indian Urbanization and Planning, Vehicles of Modernization*, Tata/ McGrawHill, New Delhi.

RRSC, (Regional Records Survey Committee Kerala State), 1970, *The History of the Freedom Movement in Kerala*, vol. 1 (*1500-1886*), Government Press, Trivandrum.

Schampers, Toon, 1984, Generation of Poverty and Coping Strategies of Coir Workers in Kerala, in *Journal of Kerala Studies*, vol. XI, part 1-4, March-December, pp. 37-63.

Schenk, Hans, 1984, Alleppey 1762-1984; Changes, Counterchanges and also Continuity, in, *Journal of Kerala Studies*, vol. XI, part 1-4, pp. 137-54.

Schenk, Hans, 2020, *Housing India's Urban Poor 1800-1965, Colonial and post-Colonial Studies*, Manohar, New Delhi.

Schenk-Sandbergen, Louise Charlotte, 1984, How to Survive without Clientele? The Impact of Social Transformation Processes on the Labour Relations of Women Domestic Servants and Coolies: A Case Study., *Journal of Kerala Studies*, vol. XI, part 1-4, pp. 23-36.

Schenk-Sandbergen, Louse Charlotte, 1988, *More or Less Work? Poverty and Survival of Female Household Servants and Their Households in Alleppey, India*, Manohar, New Delhi.

Tharakan, P. K. Michael, 1984, Socio-economic Factors in Educational Development, the Case of Nineteenth Century Travancore, in *Economic and Political Weekly*, vol. XIX, Nrs. 45 and 46. (Also: Working paper, nr. 190, Centre for Development Studies, Trivandrum.

Thomas, Jesbin Skariah, 2019, A study on Urbanisation of Kerala with Reference to the Cities and the Slum Population, in *Nagarlok*, vol. XLIX, part 4, (October-December), 2017.

Unni, K. Raman, 1969, Toward Comprehending Kerala, Some Social Perspectives for Planning Settlements, in, *Urban and Rural Planning Thoughts*, vol. XII, nr. 3-4, pp. 163-73.

Unnithan, K., Bhaskaran, 1970, *Coir Industry in India, with Special Reference to Marketing and Trade*, Cochin.

Unnithan, K. Bhaskaran, 1972, Survey for the Registration of Industrial Settlement, in *Coir*, vol. XVI, nr. 3 (April).

Varghese, T.C., 1970, *Agrarian Change and Economic Consequences: Land Tenure in Kerala 1850-1960*. Allied publishers, Bombay.

Volkart Brothers, (n.d.), 'Coir Yarn, a produce report'. Unpublished.

Woodcock, G., 1967, *Kerala, A Portrait of the Malabar Coast*, Faber & Faber, London.

Index